Learn. Pray. Do Justly.

Learn. Pray. Do Justly.

Temple Emanu–El and the American Jewish Experience

Introduction by Rabbi Eric H. Yoffie
President Emeritus, Union for Reform Judaism

Diana and Harold Cohen
Chairs, Temple Emanu-El History Committee

Edited by Susan W. Youdovin

Learn. Pray. Do Justly. Temple Emanu-El and the American Jewish Experience

Published by Temple Emanu-El
756 East Broad Street
Westfield, NJ 07090
www.tewnj.org.

© 2014 by Temple Emanu-El, Westfield NJ

All rights reserved. No part of this book may be reproduced or transmitted in any form, or by any means, electronic or mechanical, including photocopying, recording, or by any information storage and retrieval system, without permission in writing from the publisher.

For information regarding permission to reprint material from this book, please send a request in writing to Temple Emanu-El at the address listed above.

Publisher's Cataloging-in-Publication
(Provided by Quality Books, Inc.)

    Learn, pray, do justly : Temple Emanu-El and the American
      Jewish experience / introduction by Rabbi Eric H.
      Yoffie, President Emeritus, Union for Reform Judaism ;
      Diana and Harold Cohen, chairs, Temple Emanu-El History
      Committee ; edited by Susan W. Youdovin.
        pages cm
        Includes bibliographical references.
        ISBN 978-0-615-89841-4

      1. Reform Judaism—United States--History. 2. Temple
    Emanu-El (Westfield, N.J.)—History.   I. Cohen, Diana,
    1927- II. Cohen, Harold, 1926- III. Youdovin, Susan W.

     BM197.L43 2014   296.8'341'0973
                        QBI14-600005

Manufactured in the United States of America
Jacket design by Nina Ovryn Design
Art direction by Nina Ovryn Design
Copyediting by Sarah Novak
Layout and print management by Toelke Associates, Chatham NY 12037
Printed by Versa Press, Inc., East Peoria IL 61611-9788
Photo credits: Peter Byron, Steve Chernela, Charlotte Gelfand, Marvin Gershenfeld, Susan Kreitzer, Jack Rindner, Nick Romanenko

Cover images: Clockwise from upper left: Amy Levitt's first Torah; Westfield March for Soviet Jewry; *shiva minyan* volunteer; menorah, Temple Emanu-El collection

Dedicated to the generations of
Temple Emanu-El congregants,
friends, clergy, and staff
who live by the words
inscribed on our building:

To do justly

To love mercy

To walk humbly with your God

Micah 6:8

Contents

Foreword

Diana and Harold Cohen

Temple Emanu-El is the place to which we turn to learn more about Judaism, about the world, and about ourselves. Temple is our "sacred community," the safe place where we can express our inmost doubts and our deepest feelings.

We have been active members of Emanu-El for more than 50 years. Our children were educated and became b'nei mitzvah and confirmed here. Harold is a past president and celebrated his second bar mitzvah here a few years ago. At one time three members of our family were on the board of trustees at the same time.

We have been involved with five senior rabbis, two cantors, and hundreds of wonderful, dedicated lay leaders. We have chaired social action, education, and membership retention committees, served on hundreds of others, and have been involved in countless policy decisions.

In the company of our community, we have celebrated births and weddings and many other *simchas* and mourned the loss of loved ones and of major political leaders. We have watched members of our community grow from childhood to adulthood here and have watched our peers age, as we have, with gratitude for the many blessings enhanced by our longtime involvement in our joint communal enterprise, our Temple Emanu-El.

Ten years ago we were asked to chair a project, writing a history of the Temple, a continuation of the extraordinary work of Evelyn Averick, who wrote about the first 30 years in 1981. (*A Historic Narrative: The Story of Temple Emanu-El, Westfield, New Jersey. In Honor of the 30th Anniversary, 1950–1980.*) The project gradually metamorphosed into this book of essays on American Jewish life nationally and here at

Temple Emanu-El. With the help of many of you, the skillful and sensitive editor-ship of Susan Youdovin, Nina Ovryn's artful design, and Barbara Koppel's invalu-able editorial assistance, we have found a fitting way to express the special qualities of this particular synagogue, the ways in which it exemplifies and often leads in the development of the Reform Movement over the past 60 years, and how it reflects the dynamic evolution of the American Jewish community.

We hope the reader will find, as we did in working on the book, a renewed sense of pride and love for this, our synagogue, and an enhanced appreciation of the quality and dedication of our professional and lay leadership. Working together, we will continue to engage in the ongoing challenge to translate, interpret, and trans-mit the imperative to learn, pray, and do justly *l'dor v'dor*, from the past 60-plus years into twenty-first-century American Judaism.

Diana and Harold Cohen

Our Appreciation to the Editor

This volume might not have seen the light of day and certainly would not have become a significant commentary on the American Jewish experience were it not for the dedication of our editor, Susan W. Youdovin.

A longtime member of Emanu-El until she transitioned to another commu-nity, Susan has brought to this effort a lifetime of experience in the Reform Move-ment. Her knowledge of Jewish and, particularly, synagogue issues, her editorial talents and professional experience, and her leadership skills have combined to make Susan the editor we dreamed of. Most of all, we are grateful for the sensitiv-ity and love with which she has shepherded this volume.

Diana and Harold Cohen
Rabbi Charles A. Kroloff
Rabbi Douglas Sagal

Abbreviations

ARZA: Association of Reform Zionists of America

CCAR: Central Conference of American Rabbis (Reform rabbinic association)

HUC-JIR: Hebrew Union College—Jewish Institute of Religion, seminary for training Reform rabbis, cantors, educators, and lay leaders. Campuses are located in Cincinnati, Jerusalem, Los Angeles, and New York.

MRJ: Men of Reform Judaism (formerly NFTB)

NFTB: North American Federation of Temple Brotherhoods (renamed MRJ in 2007)

NFTS: North American Federation of Temple Sisterhoods (renamed WRJ in 1993)

NFTY: North American Federation of Temple Youth

TEWTY: Temple Emanu-El Westfield Temple Youth

UAHC: Union of American Hebrew Congregations (renamed URJ in 2003)

UPB: Union Prayer Book

URJ: Union for Reform Judaism, organization of Reform congregations of North America (formerly UAHC)

WRJ: Women of Reform Judaism (formerly NFTS)

WUPJ: World Union for Progressive Judaism, international body of Reform synagogues and institutions

Introduction

Rabbi Eric H. Yoffie

President Emeritus, Union for Reform Judaism

IN 1950, THE YEAR THAT TEMPLE EMANU-EL OF WESTFIELD WAS FOUNDED, AMERICAN Jews were on the move and on the threshold of dramatic change.

In the previous half century, four million Jewish immigrants had poured into the United States, mostly from Eastern Europe. The great majority of these immigrants had found a home in large American cities. But following World War II, this urban population was beginning to stir.

With the war behind them, and experiencing the first measure of prosperity, American Jews stood ready to reap the benefits bestowed upon them by immigrant parents who had slaved and sacrificed to provide them with education and every other advantage. True, American Jews were still unsure of themselves in many ways. They still faced discrimination in housing, employment, and education, and they had yet to organize and assert themselves politically as they would a generation later. Nonetheless, increasingly confident, they were looking to the future, and along with many other Americans, they began to make their way to the suburbs. And once they got there, they looked to establish new synagogues to replace the inner city *shuls* of the immigrant generation.

In the course of less than two decades, from the late 1940s to the early 1960s, American Jews became a suburban community, constructed on a foundation of suburban synagogues. And during that period, Reform Judaism, American Judaism's most progressive branch, went from being a regional movement with strong Midwestern roots to a national movement of over 700 synagogues, most of them in the rapidly growing suburban areas.

This book tells the story of one of those Reform synagogues, Temple Emanu-El of Westfield, New Jersey, founded in 1950. It is an interesting, inspiring, and important story.

More than 60 years later, that little Westfield temple has become a thriving, bustling center of synagogue activity, the largest Reform congregation in the state. And during that same period, the American Jewish community has changed beyond recognition. American Jews have left their immigrant origins far behind; no longer unsure of themselves, influential beyond their wildest dreams, the Jews of America are a proud, well-organized, and self-assured part of the American mosaic. American Reform Judaism has grown to be a movement of nearly 900 congregations and is the largest Jewish religious movement in the world.

While focusing on Temple Emanu-El, this volume also tells us a great deal about the broader Jewish community, and in particular, about the American Reform Movement. In reading its essays, almost all of which are written by those who have served as Temple Emanu-El leaders, we see that the journey from being a tiny "start-up" congregation in an overwhelmingly Christian area to a major center of Jewish life was long and difficult. We also see that Emanu-El was never a "typical" congregation, and we should remember that its success was never assured; Emanu-El grew in strength and spirit because of hard work and innovation. And while its growth and development often reflected what was happening in the Jewish world, in many ways Emanu-El both shaped and led the movement and the community of which it was a part.

Indeed, the underlying theme of this book, although the authors do not always present it this way, is that Emanu-El has been a congregation that, while committed to Jewish fundamentals, has always been open to far-reaching change. We sometimes think of synagogues as stagnant and resistant to change, but that is never true for great congregations, and it was surely not true for Emanu-El. When the Reform Movement was changing, Emanu-El was in the vanguard, often, in fact, leading the charge.

How was this change given concrete form? Let us consider what the authors of this volume tell us.

In the first place, we see that the founders of the Temple initially were, in the words of the first rabbi, "quasi-Marranos." In other words, like other Jews settling into unfamiliar suburban surroundings, they were not always accepted with open arms, and they wisely kept a low profile. But if they were to thrive and their synagogue was to thrive, they would have to fight for acceptance. Emanu-El could not prosper if Westfield was not hospitable to Jews.

And so the leaders of Emanu-El waged battles for acceptance, emphatically, but always with dignity and restraint. Thus, we read of how Temple leaders took on the Westfield Board of Education over the Christmas pageant that was a major part of the school curriculum, filing a federal lawsuit in 1972. This lawsuit generated resentment and anger, but the settlement that was reached was also a major turning point in establishing a public culture of openness and understanding in Westfield. We also read about how efforts to build a parking lot 30 years later elicited unexpected resistance and anti-Semitism, and the skillful and sensitive ways in which this resistance was overcome.

In both these cases, building coalitions with sympathetic and progressive non-Jews was essential, and these skills became the calling card of all of Emanu-El's social justice efforts. Yes, the members of Emanu-El worried about their own position, but they also knew that if Jews take care only of their own, they forget the meaning of America and of Judaism. We see how, for them, the pursuit of justice became an endless mission and a religious compulsion. Social justice did not mean talk fests, press releases, and incessant orality; it meant working with their neighbors in hands-on programs to ease the pain and change the landscape of the surrounding community. It meant housing the homeless, building ties with the local African-American community, and the extraordinary "I Have a Dream" program that helps local students in difficult circumstances find pathways to college.

A second area of change is the realm of worship and music. Emanu-El was always a Reform congregation with somewhat traditional worship patterns. Its worship services had more Hebrew than most synagogues, and its members wore *kipot*. Nonetheless, in its early days, worship was not a priority matter. But as the years passed, innovations were introduced at a startling pace. The same thing was happening elsewhere in Reform Judaism, but this is one of those areas in which Emanu-El was a pioneer, dramatically changing the synagogue's music and piloting the movement's new prayer books. Emanu-El understood, early on, that without participatory prayer and inspiring music, there would be no revival of Jewish worship, no renewal of Shabbat, and no hot passion to transform Judaism. That story, too, is told here.

A third area of change has to do with items that were simply not on the agenda when Emanu-El was founded because they were totally absent from Jewish consciousness. In 1950, the intermarriage rate among American Jews was 6%. A half-century later it was close to 50%. This required dramatic adjustments if the affected families were to retain a strong connection to the Jewish tradition, and here again, we see that the leaders of Emanu-El were prepared to take some risks and sing Jewish "notes" they had thought beyond their range. We read here about the aggressive outreach efforts of the congregation, both to encourage and embrace converts and to involve intermarried families in all areas of synagogue life. Similarly, we read about the determined efforts to bring women into all areas of Temple leadership. This was not an issue in 1950, but it was by 1970, and Emanu-El made amazing strides in encouraging gender equality; its women presidents, women clergy, *Kol Nashim* group, and active Sisterhood gave women new roles while preserving more traditional ones. At the same time, attention was paid to men's sensibilities, honoring the need for bonding and fellowship.

A fourth area of change is commitment to Israel. Israel was not absent from the agenda in the early years, but it did not emerge as a major emphasis until the Six-Day War in 1967. We read here about how, at Temple Emanu-El, the war led not only to change but also to revolution. Israel became not only an area of emphasis but the very lifeblood of the congregation. Trips to Israel were organized; Israeli speakers and students were hosted; financial support was provided; Knesset members visited regularly; some members made *aliyah*; and especially close ties were developed with the Israeli Reform Movement. Emanu-El today is a champion of Israel and Zionism; its support for Israel is proclaimed in unconditional and unmistakable tones.

We also read a number of essays about Emanu-El's impressive and creative youth and education programs, which too have evolved over the years. They deserve careful reading because, while Emanu-El is today a complex, multi-generational facility, it has always known that for a great synagogue, there are certain fundamentals upon which everything else must be built. Youth and education are two of these fundamentals. A third is a community that cares, that nurtures and sustains its members, responds to hurt and pain, and provides comfort and connectedness. This also is an area in which Emanu-El distinguishes itself, and which we read about in these pages.

Finally, there is one subject that is not really discussed in the book but is of great importance and requires special mention. Emanu-El has become a great congregation and an example to our movement and the Jewish world not only because of all the factors noted above but also because of its extraordinary rabbis. Rabbis alone do not make congregations great; devoted volunteer leaders are essential, and Emanu-El has had such leaders in abundance. But there are no great congregations without great rabbis, and in this regard, Emanu-El has been especially blessed. Its current rabbi, Doug Sagal, is a great preacher and a wonderful teacher, and above all a man of gentleness, compassion, and understanding. He is the heart and soul of Temple Emanu-El. If there is a sense of holiness that pervades every dimension of the Emanu-El community — and I believe there is — that is because Rabbi Sagal generates it with every ounce of his being, and in the process gives Jewish direction to a great institution. While I cannot mention every one of Rabbi Sagal's predecessors, I will mention one: Rabbi Charles Kroloff, my friend for 40 years, a man rooted in Torah and connected to God, a healer of souls and a reassuring voice of calm, both a national leader of Reform Judaism and a great congregational rabbi who did more than anyone else to prepare the ground on which Rabbi Sagal now walks.

Temple Emanu-El is an exceptional and unique Reform congregation. It is a synagogue that recognizes the diversity of needs that exist in congregations today and one that provides its members with multiple gates of entry into the Jewish people and the Jewish faith. In reading this volume, we learn about its strengths and its struggles, about the great issues of the Jewish world, and about how Jews today search out human holiness. It is a must-read for all who are serious about understanding American Jewry and the challenges of American Jewish life.

PART I

In the
Community

LEARN. PRAY. DO JUSTLY.

CHAPTER ONE

Social Action:
In Temple Emanu-El's "DNA"

Introduction

Diana and Harold Cohen, Jacqui Rose
Temple Emanu-El

W E AT TEMPLE EMANU-EL HAVE ALWAYS VIEWED SOCIAL ACTION AS THE PROCESS of translating the principles of Judaism into action at home and in the broader community. Whether helping to house the homeless or marching in support of oppressed communities throughout the world, Jewish and non-Jewish alike, we continually seek to bridge the gap between prayer and practice, creed and conduct.

With a deep belief in prophetic Judaism, Jack Rindner advocated strongly for Temple Emanu-El to become an engine for social justice in the 1960s. Returning from the March on Washington for Jobs and Freedom, he and Alan Goldstein led the fight for fair housing in Westfield and, together with Harold and Diana Cohen, initiated a relationship with the leadership of the African-American Cacciola Place community. The clear priority of that community was to help their children get a good education in the Westfield schools. An ambitious tutoring program was quickly established. Temple Emanu-El provided volunteer tutors, classroom space, and drivers. Other church groups joined in the effort and eventually took over the project.

Alan and Rabbi Kroloff then took on the task of providing low-income housing in the community. The relationship continues to this day, with Harold Cohen still serving as president of the Westfield Neighborhood Council.

Although the Temple board did not always sanction our efforts in those early days of the civil rights movement, we persisted with grape and lettuce boycotts and demonstrations in support of Cesar Chavez and the Farm Workers Union. Harris Gilbert was appointed social action chair and became so committed he went on to head the national URJ (then UAHC) Commission on Social Action and the advocacy group, Common Cause New Jersey.

Given our deep convictions, it is not surprising that a commitment to social action would be a key attribute for any rabbi we would select. We have been very fortunate in the leadership provided by Rabbi Kroloff, Rabbi Sagal, and our student, assistant, and associate rabbis on this issue.

Two of those former student rabbis, Rabbi Joel Soffin and Rabbi Lennard Thal, shared their perspectives with us for this book. Rabbi Soffin writes about our "Jewish Tattoo," how we are called to perform *mitzvot*. He also describes the critical role of social justice as an entry point for people of every generation, especially the young. Rabbi Thal recounts his experience with the first Temple Emanu-El public demonstration in Westfield, the March in Support of Soviet Jewry.

We are highlighting four signature programs that express Temple Emanu-El's commitment to social justice and have achieved enduring results — the Interfaith Hospitality Network for the homeless (now known as Family Promise); ARK, Association for Rehabilitation with Kindness; "I Have a Dream"; and the Mitzvah Garden.

Temple Emanu-El also offers Blankets of Love, handmade afghans for children with cancer attending summer camp, and two programs to help combat hunger. The Mandy Reichman Feeding Program, staffed by a core group of adults and a favorite b'nei mitzvah project, prepares bag lunches each week for neighborhoods in nearby Elizabeth. Confirmation classes participate in Bridges, an outreach program that delivers food, toiletries, and clothing to people in need in surrounding communities. Three times a year, Emanu-El teens gather for "Sandwiches and Study" to learn about Jewish approaches to hunger and prepare three hundred to five hundred bag lunches for personal delivery.

We fulfill ourselves as Jews by working for the establishment of justice and peace for Jews throughout the world and for all oppressed people. What does God expect of us? Temple Emanu-El continues to answer, "To do justly, love mercy, and walk humbly with [our] God."

The Jewish Tattoo on our Foreheads

Rabbi Joel E. Soffin

President and Founder, Jewish Helping Hands Foundation
Temple Emanu-El Student Rabbi/Youth Director 1973–76

WHEN PEOPLE ASK ME WHEN I STARTED BECOMING ACTIVELY INVOLVED IN SOCIAL action and social justice issues, I refer to a conversation that I had with Rob Cohen, then a member of our Temple Emanu-El Senior Youth Group, as a turning point.

It was 1973, and I was brand new to Westfield. In getting to know the area, I drove along Route 22 and passed a place called Bowcraft, which offered, among other amusements, baseball batting cages. I must say that I used to love those batting cages, and I was really looking forward to going there. So you can understand my dismay when Rob asked me if I had heard about the boycotts. Boycotts, I thought to myself, what boycotts? Rob explained that we supported Cesar Chavez and the United Farm Workers Union by not eating non-union lettuce, and that we didn't patronize Bowcraft, which was owned by members of the John Birch Society.

We are taught in our tradition (Babylonian Talmud *Yevamot* 79a) that our people can be described as *rachmanim b'nei rachmanim* — the merciful descendants of merciful ancestors. This is a way we define ourselves. The Hebrew word *rachmanim* is related to the word *rechem,* meaning womb. It is as if we take in our concern for others *in utero.* When we see people in need, when we hear about people who try to help them, we are drawn to be among them. Whether we realize it or not, for us as Jews, this is a deep ancestral calling. Since my years at Temple Emanu-El, I have witnessed that call being answered by Jews of all ages with great enthusiasm and eagerness, and I believe that this will be a basis of Judaism and Jewish life in the future as well.

There were the young b'nei mitzvah students, searching for meaningful, personal *tzedakah* projects, ready to exceed our expectations of them. One became the leader of the Chickens for El Salvador project, a 12-year-old interacting with rabbis and educators around the country. Another collected and organized all of the school supplies and clothing that we would bring into Cambodia as we traveled to dedicate the middle school we have had built and were now endowing. When he asked his mother if they, too, could go to Cambodia, she responded immediately, "Yes, let's go," and they did.

In 2004, when I created the Million Quarter Project, teenagers played a very significant role. This project was designed to provide one million meals for hungry Ethiopian Jewish children, still in Ethiopia, awaiting permission from the Israeli government to immigrate. Each meager lunchtime meal, which was almost all the food the children would eat that day, consisted of a roll, a piece of carrot, some beans, an orange, a potato, and, if there was extra money, an egg.

The national Reform Movement was initially uninterested in supporting this project. So I went to a regional conclave with my youth group president, and we made a pitch to the teenagers. They immediately agreed to add $1 to the cost of every one of their events. That was a very positive response, but it was not enough.

They needed to go to the board of the URJ and to challenge the adults to join in too. The teens were eager to do so and, due in large part to their efforts, very soon thereafter, it became an international project. Two years later, we had collected 1,100,000 quarters!

Researchers have discovered that such social action projects are among the most appealing Jewish entry points for young people, including those in their 20s and 30s. They require little previous Jewish education or Hebrew or prayer skills — just a willing heart, a giving soul, and a chance to make a real difference helping others.

But that's not the end of the process. It's just the beginning. Out of their sincere and, I would say, Jewish desire to help, these young people eagerly join what have become known as service learning projects. One example is *Bonim Banim*: Building Youth, a weeklong summer experience we created for those entering grades nine and ten. Some signed up to help reconfigure the home of a Maine woman soon to be wheelchair-bound, others to restore a Massachusetts residential recovery center for 30 women, but all soon realize that this is really an experience in Jewish religious living.

They pray each morning and study Torah each night and, when they return home, they are different. One participant said that he would now return to Confirmation, join the youth group, and go on the rabbi's next trip to Israel. Social action became the doorway to fuller involvement in Jewish life. And he was not alone.

It isn't just the younger generations that feel this calling to help. It is felt by all of our generations. Several years ago in the immediate aftermath of Hurricane Katrina, I led a group of some 35 volunteers from *Tzevet Mitzvot*, the Reform Movement's Adult Mitzvah Corps, on the first of three trips to New Orleans to help rebuild severely damaged houses.

The following December at a Men's Club breakfast in Franklin Lakes, New Jersey, I spoke of how we had helped to restore the homes of four Jewish families. In the course of my presentation, I explained that I believe that each of us has a mitzvah, a *tzedakah* project, tattooed on his or her forehead. If that is so, then one of the challenges of our lives is to discover what that mitzvah is. When we do discover it, an amazing thing will happen: without any prodding or guilt or sermon, we will immediately feel compelled to fulfill it. Nothing will be able to hold us back. We will know that we have been called, that one of our purposes on earth is to perform this mitzvah.

I like to imagine that some people have a mirror. When you meet them and they tell you about some of the many *tzedakah* opportunities that exist in our world, as Rob Cohen did for me, they are holding the mirror up before our faces. Sometimes, in that mirror we can see our tattoo, and then miracles begin to happen.

As I was speaking to that Men's Club group, someone in the back of the room raised his hand and said, "I'm going with you on your next trip to New Orleans." Now I had not been asking for volunteers to join me on our second building project there. I was just relating to the men some of the work I'd been involved in. I explained that to him, but he kept insisting that he was going with me to New Orleans.

Finally, I stopped and asked him why he was so sure about this. He was quick to respond, as he said in a quiet voice, "I'm going because that's the mitzvah tattooed on my forehead." "How can you be so sure?" I asked. And this is what he said: "I'm a carpenter by trade. In all the years that I have worked on building houses, I never felt that my work had any great meaning or holiness. Now I know that it can, so I'm going with you to New Orleans."

And of course, he went with us that year and returned the following one, too. Not only that, he is now serving as one of our building experts, supervising the *Bonim Banim* projects. Nothing can hold him back from joining in or from participating now in Talmud study, too.

This is not a new idea. In the Talmud, in *Tractate Shabbat* (118b-119a), we find a group of rabbis praying for special rewards because they were particularly good at fulfilling a specific mitzvah. One never walked more than four cubits bare-headed; another always prayed with great *kavanah*, with deep devotion; and a third never failed to eat three special meals on Shabbat. Each one knew that he had found his tattoo.

Was that carpenter the only one who has recognized his tattoo and had such a holy experience? Far from it.

As we were beginning the Million Quarter Project, I remembered the father of a recent bar mitzvah boy who had told me that his business was making cardboard boxes. So I called him and asked if he could make cardboard quarter holders like the ones the March of Dimes used to have. He carefully explained to me the nature of his business. The kind of cardboard he used was different from that needed for quarter holders. His production line couldn't produce such things anyway, and he was in the process of moving his plant, which entailed all kinds of new government regulations and inspections. "No, Rabbi, it wouldn't be possible."

I thanked him for considering it and for talking to me, and the conversation ended. It wasn't five minutes later that the phone rang. He was calling back. All excited, he asked, "Can you take fifty thousand quarter holders? That's my smallest run."

What had happened in those five minutes? He had seen his tattoo.

And then there was the businessman who donated warehouse space and a courier service, the printer who donated all of the posters, the webmaster who created the website, the camp arts and crafts counselor who created quarter holders for the campers to wear on their belts, and so many more.

No one had to tell them to do these things; they just knew it was their mitzvah, and they felt commanded to fulfill it. They had the skills, the ideas, the capacity to make the world a little better, and one by one they came through for those hungry Ethiopian children.

None of them saw what they were doing as being a burden or a hassle. They were thankful for the chance to help, and they wanted to do more and more. Their families and friends were drawn in as well. New energy was released, and everyone felt empowered and uplifted. They realized that this was a unique opportunity for holiness and a chance to do God's work. Such experiences are repeated every day throughout the Jewish world.

Studies by David Elcott[1] and others have revealed that Jewish baby boomers, representing 50 percent of the affiliated Jews in the United States, are eager to add meaningful activities to their lives. He notes that they have a strong Jewish identity and would prefer to find such experiences within the Jewish world, but "if the Jewish community doesn't provide meaning for them, they will go elsewhere." According to *The Jewish Week*, he stated, "We are not prepared for that. We're prepared for it from our 30-year-olds, but not from this middle generation."[2] Linda Blumberg, planning director for the Jewish Federation of Metropolitan Detroit, has said, "If we lose this generation, we lose their children and grandchildren."[3]

While social action is not the only such entry point, it is the one with the lowest threshold that meets young and old Jews alike closest to where they are in their Jewish strivings and interests.

On the second work day at one of our Adult Mitzvah Corps builds, the kind that Temple Emanu-El's Jeanne Goldstein and Hannah and Steve Lieberman have attended, a local television station interviewed some of the participants. One was asked, "Why are you here?"

Two nights before at our orientation meeting, many had said that they were there because it was a cheap vacation or a challenge from friends or because they didn't believe we could build a whole house in five days. Neither God nor Torah nor *mitzvot* were mentioned. Now, just two days later, this participant said, "I'm here because it's a mitzvah, a commandment. I feel that God wants me to be here."

Together, we learn that our tradition teaches that God can be found standing next to the poor and the needy (*Midrash Rabba Ruth 5:9*). The participants in social action may not be seeking to be in God's presence, but they quickly recognize when they have been. Entering Jewish life through these acts of helping, they have found a renewed sense of spirituality and Torah.

And there's more.

A few years ago, we discovered that there were homeless people living in tents in the Lakewood area. A caravan of SUVs, filled with the things they needed, drove there and met the "residents." We had brought much more than could be used immediately. The rest was stored at a nearby church.

One SUV driver was a lawyer whose father had been homeless during the Depression. He committed his firm to do *pro bono* work on behalf of the people there. Before long, he had contacted the appropriate social service agencies, acquainting them with the presence of these poor people. The agencies began to provide help to them. He went further and arranged to rent an apartment for the weakest and the pregnant to use. Then he appeared before the local town council to advocate for shelters to be provided. The case is in the courts, but system change is a likely outcome. Hands-on social action work is leading to advocacy as well.

So it is clear to me that social action is a vital key to the future vibrancy of Jewish life. The research demonstrates the deep Jewish concern that all of our generations have. All they need is to be shown the doorway and welcomed in. There is no time to lose.

This urgency is clear in the social action blessing that was chosen by the Reform Movement. Traditionally, there is no such blessing. After reciting a blessing, we would immediately perform the mitzvah. But what if the intended recipient refuses to accept our offer of help? Then it would be a *brachah l'vatalah*, a blessing in vain, since we would be unable to fulfill it. And what if the person in need cannot wait for us to take the time to remember the words of the blessing and then to recite it? What if her need is too urgent and great? Better not to say a blessing at all.

In the light of all of this, the Reform Movement's choice of wording for the blessing is especially significant. It ends with the words *lirdof tzedek*, acknowledging that God has commanded us to "pursue" justice. That doesn't mean that we have to "catch up" to every act of *tzedek*, but it does mean that we can't stop trying, that we can't stop looking for opportunities to perfect the world. And, in some ways, that we are programmed, hard-wired, to do so.

Indeed, there are times when God seems to be giving us a little nudge to keep us going. It's the day of the first seder. I'm rushing to buy *afikoman* gifts. As I speed walk along Broadway, I pass a man sitting on the curb begging. Two things are unusual about him, even in Manhattan. He's wearing a *kipah*, and he asks me if I have $26 to give him. $26?! I wonder about that number as I continue on my way. I pass two more people asking for help. I don't stop for them either, but I promise myself that I will give them some money on my way back.

After I complete my errand, I retrace my steps. I find the two beggars and help them. Then suddenly I realize that 26 is the *gematria* (numerical) value of the Hebrew letters in the four-letter name of God. As I look earnestly for that man from street to street without ever finding him, I realize that I had missed something important. Perhaps he was Elijah the prophet, looking for a welcoming hand and a place at the seder table.

The ancestral call of *tzedakah* seems to be getting louder and louder. All of our generations are hearing it and are eager to respond. It has always been so. If we, in the organized Jewish community, can hear it, too, if we can see the *mitzvot* tattooed on our own foreheads and serve as mirrors to others, then the Jewish people and its future will be much more secure.

Marching for Soviet Jewry:
A First for Temple Emanu-El

Rabbi Lennard Thal

URJ Senior Vice President Emeritus; Temple Emanu-El Student Rabbi, 1970–1973

IN THE FALL OF 1970, JEWS AROUND THE UNITED STATES WERE BECOMING AWARE OF an increasingly dramatic story unfolding in the USSR, a story reflecting some indications that our courageous Jewish brothers and sisters there were awakening to the possibility of embracing their Jewish heritage and legacy. Indeed, the bravest among them were risking their livelihood by speaking out and, even more audaciously, by petitioning the Soviet authorities to let them leave for Israel, the United States, or elsewhere.

Temple Emanu-El had acquitted itself well in the 1960s in other arenas of social justice, especially with respect to the civil rights movement and opposition to our involvement in the war in Vietnam. Of course, the civil rights movement had evolved throughout the 1960s. By the end of that decade and beginning of the next, it was no longer a matter of Jews going to the South to participate in voter registration efforts, but rather (and more typically), to work to assure matters of fair housing locally in the Westfield area and to enable teenage members of the congregation to participate in the various URJ (then UAHC) Urban Mitzvah Corps programs in New Jersey, California, and elsewhere.

At the same time, the congregation had amassed an enviable record of Israel support, not just financial but programmatic as well. So, there was a sense of Jewish peoplehood in the community, though a strong tie to Israel may have been the extent of it. The question that arose in 1970 was how to respond to the headlines being generated by the Student Struggle for Soviet Jewry and other new and existing organizations working to support the reawakened expressions of Jewish identity in a country that had repressed religion under the rule of the Communist governments for more than 50 years.

Prompted by the partnering of Rabbi Charles Kroloff and some stalwart lay leaders, including Annette and Jack Rindner, Sally and Harris Gilbert, Jeanne and Alan Goldstein, Diana and Harold Cohen, Lois and Gerry Staffin, and others, a decision was made to mount a public statement of support so that not just the congregation but other citizens of Westfield would get the clear message that Temple Emanu-El was firmly supportive of Soviet Jews. Further, it was determined that this meant taking the statement to the streets of Westfield, a "first" for the community, and to do so at the end of December 1970. Since Rabbi Kroloff had longstanding plans to be out of town at that time, it fell to me as Temple Emanu-El's rabbinic student intern to "staff" the event.

It is important to remember that by 1970, the congregation had been a presence in Westfield for fewer than 20 years, and the community had proved less than welcoming. Westfield High School had featured a major Christmas program for quite a period of time, a program whose clear religious orientation made our community sufficiently uncomfortable that Temple Emanu-El members ultimately were instrumental in the legal proceedings that brought that tradition to an end. Whereas it is said in some quarters that "children should be seen and not heard," there was a view held by some in that era that that statement also ought to be applied to Westfield's Jews, and there were those who were not so sure they should even be "seen" as a community outside their synagogue at 756 East Broad.

Although some in the Emanu-El community were hesitant, still we determined that it was sufficiently important to express public support for Soviet Jews that we should organize a march from the Temple down the residential portion of East Broad to Mindowaskin Park, complete with placards and, as I recall, certain vocal expressions of support. Of course, since this was to happen one early evening on the principal street of the town, precautions were necessary so as not to disturb the peace. Indeed, we needed to notify the local police in advance; in turn, they made sure to be present throughout the march. Such public demonstrations were hardly commonplace in Colonial Westfield!

Perhaps as much as any other event in the Temple's history, this march illustrated the congregation's ability to express support and solidarity not only in the various social justice arenas that characterized the decade now completed but to do so in a Jewishly particularistic manner as well. Simply stated, Temple Emanu-El's congregants had come to understand that we not only felt compelled to respond to the universal imperative of our Biblical prophets but also that we needed (and need) to embrace the notion of *Kol Yisrael arevim zeh b'zeh* — "All Israel is responsible one for the other."

Postscript: Evelyn Averick's account of the march notes this is "the first public demonstration the Temple ever had . . . creating a major impact on the larger community and on Westfield Jewry. Ministerium and public officials participated along with a responsive and determined crowd of several hundred people."[4] A strong program of support for Soviet Jewry, both personal and institutional, followed. Temple Emanu-El has since championed the cause of the oppressed in many countries, from Ethiopian and Syrian Jewish communities to Darfur and elsewhere.

Temple Emanu-El Programs in Action

Jacqui Rose
Temple Emanu-El

Rabbi Charles Kroloff
Temple Emanu-El Rabbi Emeritus

Rabbi Erin Glazer
Temple Emanu-El Associate Rabbi

Four signature programs characterize Temple Emanu-El's ongoing commitment to social action — the Interfaith Hospitality Network (now known as Family Promise); ARK, the Association for Rehabilitation with Kindness; "I Have a Dream"; and the Mitzvah Garden. All four exemplify Emanu-El volunteers' "Jewish Tattoo."

Interfaith Hospitality Network (IHN)

IN 1985 KAREN OLSON BEGAN GIVING OUT SANDWICHES TO THE HOMELESS MEN AND women she encountered at the Port Authority Bus Terminal in New York during her commute from Summit, New Jersey. Feeling called to do more, Karen mobilized the religious and social service communities of Union County to provide shelter and services for homeless families.

In October 1986, the Interfaith Council for the Homeless of Union County welcomed its first guests into the Interfaith Hospitality Network (IHN). Initially, 11 Union County congregations hosted up to 15 adults and children for a week at a time on a rotating basis. IHN became a model for the religious community throughout the country.

Jacqui Rose, Lauren Shub, Gerry Cantor, Bernard Weinstein, Roz Helfen, Randi Feiner, Rabbi Kroloff, and others advocated for Temple Emanu-El to become part of this innovative outreach and helped shape the program. Despite the fact that guests were primarily women and children or men who were part of a family, some Temple members had issues with a "homeless" population living in the building. The advocates ultimately prevailed. Emanu-El hosted its first group of families in November 1986, the first synagogue in the region to do so.

The response was immediate and overwhelmingly positive. More than three hundred members volunteered to donate clothing, bedding, toys, gifts, and other supplies, prepare and serve dinner, play with the children of the guest families, stay overnight at the synagogue, and provide other services as needed. Volunteers from St. Mark's Episcopal Church in Plainfield, Emanu-El's partner congregation through ARK, also participated in the shelter program.

Emanu-El members were deeply engaged in more than just hosting. Gerry Cantor served as president of the IHN of Union County, Lauren Shub headed Volunteer Resources, and Jacqui Rose was instrumental in many aspects of the program. With the encouragement of Adam Bengal, Rabbi Kroloff was inspired to write *When Elijah Knocks: A Religious Response to Homelessness* in 1992.[5] Rabbi Arnold Gluck, an associate rabbi at Emanu-El when the program began, successfully adapted the program to Somerset County.

Home First, an organization that arose from the IHN experience, now focuses on the purchase and rehabilitation of houses in Plainfield to serve as transitional housing as well as support services for vulnerable individuals and families.

IHN Founder Karen Olson has expanded the IHN concept across America through a national initiative known as Family Promise (www.familypromise.org). The program now includes 182 IHN affiliates in 41 states with more than 160,000 volunteers who have served over 550,000 guests. Temple Emanu-El, one of the 12 original IHN congregations, has signed on to partner with Family Promise in order to help reinvigorate the Union County shelter network.

The Association for Rehabilitation with Kindness:
The "ARK Angels"

IN THE 1980s, THE BOND BETWEEN JEWISH AND AFRICAN-AMERICAN COMMUNITIES forged during the civil rights protests of the 1960s had become strained. Temple Emanu-El member Sally Gilbert, a social worker in the Plainfield schools, saw an opportunity to change the dynamic. Her vision, and the longtime leadership of Emanu-El's Jacqui Rose, led to an ongoing relationship between Plainfield's St. Mark's Episcopal Church and Emanu-El, their congregants, and spiritual leaders.

The two congregations initiated a dialogue in 1985. By the following year, 150 people had joined forces to produce the Broadway musical *The Pajama Game*. A multiracial cast with alternating leads from each congregation gave four performances at Plainfield High School to packed houses. The performances raised $7,000 for the Interfaith Council for the Homeless. In the process, members of the two congregations got to know each other, had fun, and forged ongoing friendships

As the relationship continued to flourish through dialogue, visits to each other's worship services, pulpit exchanges between Rabbi Kroloff and Father (now Canon) Leroy Lyons, and social get-togethers, the two congregations formalized their relationship. They created ARK, the Association for Rehabilitation with Kindness, a non-profit corporation that "seeks to build bridges of understanding between these faith-based communities through shared activities."

While ARK continued its wide-ranging inter-congregational activities, the organization's signature activity became the rehabilitation of rundown homes in basically sound Plainfield neighborhoods. To date, 40 houses have been rehabilitated for grateful homeowners in need of help. One Plainfield woman called the team "my ARK angels!"

In 1989, ARK won the first Kovler Award for Black-Jewish Relations, presented by the URJ Religious Action Center in Washington. ARK has also been awarded grants by the Martin Luther King Commemorative Committee, the Westfield Foundation, and the Plainfield Foundation.

"I Have a Dream"

In 2000, Rabbi Kroloff and Temple Emanu-El member Warren Eisenberg set out to discover a way to help more students in the neighboring city of Plainfield find pathways to college. They discovered the national "I Have a Dream" Foundation and were inspired by their program, mission, and goals. With the encouragement of Plainfield's then superintendent of schools, Dr. Larry Leverett, and Clinton School's principal, Dr. Kenneth Hamilton, the entire first grade was adopted. Warren Eisenberg promised the students that if they graduated from high school, he would provide the "last dollars" in tuition to make it possible for them to continue on to college and other post-secondary education.

An on-site program director was engaged to build relationships with students and families, work alongside teachers, and generally guide these students' development over the years. Volunteers were sought from Temple Emanu-El as well as ARK partner St. Mark's Episcopal Church of Plainfield. A board of trustees was established, led by Temple members Susan Jacobson (2000–05), Susan Pepper (2000–present), and Don Wortzel (2005–present).

The project began with afternoon programs of homework help and opportunities for cultural enrichment, and continued with summer programs to have fun and advance academic skills, along with trips to museums, plays, concerts, and sporting events. Counseling, mentoring, academic support, SAT preparation, and guidance for post–high school choices were also provided.

Some two hundred Temple Emanu-El volunteers have touched the lives of the 57 Dreamers. Program Coordinator Larry Johnson and the board of trustees will continue to support and counsel the students as they proceed through college.

In 2012 the overwhelming majority of Dreamers graduated from high school and embarked on their college education, more than double the number normally achieved in Plainfield. Students have been accepted to such schools as The College of New Jersey, Montclair State University, Pennsylvania State University, Johnson and Wales, Seton Hall University, The College of St. Elizabeth, St. Peter's University, Rider University, Middlesex Community College, and Union County College.

Mitzvah Garden

When you reap the harvest of your land,
you shall not reap all the way to the edges of your field,
or gather the gleanings of your harvest;
you shall leave them for the poor and the stranger.

LEVITICUS 23:22

When Temple Emanu-El Associate Rabbi Erin Glazer delivered a High Holy Day sermon in 2010 about feeding the hungry from the corners of our fields, congregants took it to heart. In the summer of 2012, Emanu-El Mitzvah Garden volunteers harvested their first crop — 38 heads of lettuce, followed by zucchini, tomatoes, and carrots. The fresh produce was delivered to the Westfield Food Pantry where it was distributed to people who do not get enough to eat, especially fresh vegetables.

The Biblical injunction was fulfilled in a modern way. Everyone in the congregation, from toddlers to seniors, could engage with the Mitzvah Garden. Temple Emanu-El Early Childhood Education (ECE) students helped plant the first crop and are in charge of watering the garden, centrally located in the Temple courtyard where everyone entering the synagogue can see it. Garden team leaders Eleanor Peris, John Delesio-Blumenreich, Danielle Levitt, Hannah Lieberman, Tracey McColly, and David Judd, with support from Shep Federgreen, the Emanu-El president at the time, developed the project, brought it to fruition, and continue to manage it.

The Mitzvah Garden also provides opportunities for teaching ECE and Religious School children Jewish values around the environment, feeding the hungry, and taking care of the community. Grandparents, grandchildren, and everyone in between help tend the garden; one family donated heirloom tomato seedlings.

The goal is to infuse social action into every aspect of Temple Emanu-El life, both the value and the doing of it. The Mitzvah Garden is a beautiful example of how Emanu-El's own "fields" can make a real difference for the Temple's neighbors.

Chapter Notes

1. "Baby Boomers, Public Service and Minority Communities: A Case Study of the Jewish Community in the United States." Cited in Naomi Zeveloff, "New Push to Link Jewish Boomers to Community," *The Jewish Daily Forward*, July 29, 2011. http://forward.com/articles/140151/new-push-to-link-jewish-boomers-to-community/

2. Sue Fishkoff, JTA, "What About the Jewish Baby Boomers?" *The Jewish Week*, November 8, 2010. http://www.thejewishweek.com/news/national/what_about_jewish_baby_boomers

3. Ibid.

4. Evelyn Averick, *A Historic Narrative: The Story of Temple Emanu-El, Westfield, New Jersey. In Honor of the 30th Anniversary, 1950–1980* (May 1981), 79–80.

5. Rabbi Charles A. Kroloff, *When Elijah Knocks: A Religious Response to Homelessness* (West Orange, N.J.: Behrman House, 1992).

CHAPTER TWO

Temple Emanu-El and Westfield Overcoming Challenges: A Christmas Pageant and a Parking Lot

W ITH THE EXCEPTION OF A HANDFUL OF FAMILIES AND LOCAL STORE OWNERS, the Jewish population of Westfield was practically nonexistent in the early 1950s. As was true in many other suburbs, the Jewish population grew with the postwar movement of the population to the suburbs, seeking better lives for their families.

Westfield was not very hospitable to Jews in the early 1950s. Rabbi Ezra Spicehandler, Temple Emanu-El's first spiritual leader, described the Jews in Westfield as "quasi-Marranos."[1] Many Westfield neighborhoods, particularly the North Side, were closed to Jews. Families who wanted to buy there were told they "would not feel comfortable."

When Jewish families sought to establish a synagogue, a committee of neighbors objected and prepared to petition the town council. The Reverend Joseph Lyle McCorison Jr., pastor of the First Congregational Church of Westfield, offered the families a home and effectively stopped the petition. The fledgling congregation met in the church's parish house until 1953 when the synagogue was completed. It was built on the only parcel of land anyone was willing to sell to the synagogue, a lot owned by Sam Weintraub, a local Jewish druggist who moved ahead with the sale despite vehement objections and threats of a boycott.[2]

As more families moved to Westfield, many began to challenge the status quo. Accustomed to the diverse cultures and strong Jewish presence in New York, Newark, and Elizabeth, Jews encountered a community that was primarily Christian. The annual Christmas pageant at Westfield High School became a lightning rod for controversy and, ultimately, the catalyst for far-reaching change.

The Christmas Pageant

Lynn and Bernard Turiel
Temple Emanu-El

FOR MANY YEARS WESTFIELD HIGH SCHOOL PRODUCED "ART MASTERPIECES," A Christmas pageant that was artistically put together, a series of tableaus of religious paintings accompanied by religious music. When the "Hallelujah Chorus" from Handel's *Messiah* was sung, the audience followed the old English tradition, standing and refraining from applause. Many felt this behavior was more appropriate for a church service than a school program.

Students who wanted to take the highly acclaimed chorus course were compelled to participate in the pageant. The same was true for art, drama, and instrumental music students, all of whom spent the entire fall semester preparing for the event. Diana and Harold Cohen's son Allen, the chorus accompanist, refused to participate and was forced to sit out the semester.

Many in the Westfield community, both Jews and Christians, objected to this program and voiced their opposition, but positions hardened. In 1972 Muriel Hyman, a member of Temple Emanu-El, together with leaders throughout the Jewish and non-Jewish community, formed CARES, Committee Against the Religious Encroachment in Schools, to oppose the pageant.

CARES, comprising nearly 180 members of the Westfield community, Christians as well as Jews, joined as plaintiffs in a federal lawsuit against the Board of Education. The suit claimed the pageant violated the separation of church and state clause of the First Amendment of the US Constitution.

The action engendered great turmoil in Westfield. Rabbi Kroloff appealed to the local clergy but was met mostly with silence. Others in town were not so silent. There were references in the *Westfield Leader* to the "strangers in our midst" who were trying to change the way things were done in town and threats of boycotts against Jewish merchants. Jewish doctors lost patients. As the atmosphere became increasingly ugly, Jewish parents feared a backlash of anti-Semitism directed at their school-age children, and many walked them to and from school each day.

Ultimately, CARES attorneys Alan Goldstein and Bernard Turiel appeared before Judge Frederick B. Lacey of the US District Court in Newark. He urged both sides to get together and resolve the matter. A Committee of Six, three representatives from the Board of Education and three from CARES, worked out a compromise that formed the basis of a consent order that was legally binding on all parties.

According to the *Westfield Leader*, "Both sides said that consideration of the sensitivities and religious convictions of all the people of Westfield were considered in coming to the following provisions in the consent order."[3] The first provision specified that "Art Masterpieces" would no longer be presented in its current form, nor would any Westfield schools present programs "the purpose or effect of which is the advancement of any religion or all religions." The second provision did not prohibit holiday programs in the schools from including "appropriate choral or instrumental music, drama, art, tableaus, dance, or other art forms." CARES attorneys noted the importance of learning about all religions, and Board of Education President George A. Plenty concurred that "holiday programs should promote understanding." CARES voted to accept the consent order as did eight of the nine members of the Board of Education.

Despite the objections of the Westfield Citizens' Organization, which presented a petition to Judge Lacey supporting the traditional Christmas program, the consent order was approved. It was not a question of numbers, Judge Lacey noted, but of law. "Now, I have with pride seen my children over the years participate in holiday programs," he added. "I firmly believe that given good will and understanding on the part of both sides, these programs can continue in Westfield. I believe they can be put into a learning concept and not a teaching-of-religion concept. I believe that thus directed, programs such as this play a vital role in a child's education."[4]

In the course of discussions leading up to the settlement, school officials agreed to make changes in the program. However, CARES was not at all optimistic that the Board of Education would agree to substantial changes. In the end, the pageant was dropped altogether, and Jewish children in the town's schools felt no repercussions.

The settlement of the pageant litigation was a major breakthrough in this community. Many members of the board itself seem to have understood that the program was inappropriate in a public school but did not want to invite controversy by making this decision unilaterally, especially because some members of the board were rabid supporters of the pageant. Any attempt from within to eliminate the pageant would deeply divide the community, as was borne out by reactions to the lawsuit. In the end, the settlement was even well-received by the many teachers at the high school who were unhappy with the program, as it had required them to give their full attention to pageant preparation for an entire semester.

While this was a deeply divisive and painful period for the Jewish community in Westfield, it signaled a turning point. The initiatives and inspiration over the years of our great lay leaders, as well as Rabbi Kroloff and Rabbi Sagal, have enabled the Jewish population to flourish and become an integral part of a more open and hospitable Westfield community.

The Parking Lot

Stephen E. Barcan
Temple Emanu-El

As Temple Emanu-El grew, the synagogue recognized that it needed an expanded parking lot. The goal was to move cars off the street, creating a safer environment for Temple-goers and for our neighbors. Simply stated, uneven sidewalks were a concern for many members, particularly older members, walking at night. An opportunity arose to buy the property next door. The property was a large lot with a dilapidated house and provided ample room for a parking lot expansion. Rabbi Kroloff and Temple leadership, including the committee formed for this purpose, discussed the potential community reaction to a parking lot. The feeling was that while the Rabbi Charles A. Kroloff Center for Jewish Learning then under Planning Board review would enlarge the building, it would be on the same footprint and within the property; it would attract attention but would be approved. The parking lot, however, was an expansion outside the Temple property and for that reason alone would likely generate significant and strong opposition that might raise issues going back years. Balanced against that was the fact that an opportunity to acquire such a large, contiguous parcel would never come our way again, and so the purchase moved ahead.

The parking lot committee was co-chaired by past president Bob Koppel and board member Laurie Goldsmith-Heitner. In my capacity as a past president and land use attorney who has represented many houses of worship, I also served on the committee. Then-president Steve Rosenberg, Rabbi Sagal, and committee members met with neighbors to discuss the project well in advance of formal plans being prepared and submitted to the Town. The Temple felt that neighbors' concerns about traffic, noise, visual impact, lighting, and other issues were taken into account as site plans were developed, but opposition remained.

In January 2003, the Board of Adjustment scheduled the first public hearing on the Temple's request for the required zoning variances. The variance request sparked a major controversy, stretching into a year of hearings, including special meetings. Those who had weathered the Christmas pageant debate and thought that attitudes had changed were probably surprised at the reaction. People who had come to Westfield after the 1970s were probably shocked.

While adjacent residents aired some legitimate concerns about lighting, landscaping, traffic patterns (for example, backups on Broad Street when children were being picked up), and other issues at both informal and public meetings, others from inside and outside the neighborhood used the occasion for vitriolic, anti-Semitic attacks. An opposition group formed, calling itself UNITE (United Neighbors Investigating Temple Expansion). UNITE placed inflammatory ads in the *Westfield Leader* decrying "overdevelopment." The ads said, "In *colonial Westfield* where practically all houses of worship, businesses and commuters have parking shortages, THIS IS NOT A SOLUTION!" Others urged, "Don't pave paradise and put up a Parking Lot!!"[5]

The public hearings, which drew large crowds, continued through the year. UNITE hired an attorney. Public comment on two consecutive evenings continued for hours. Rabbi Sagal, Rabbi Kroloff, and Executive Director Carolyn Shane testified and were questioned about such things as the Temple's expansion plans (there were none), how many people used the building each day, how many members lived out of town, and how many civic events were held at the Temple. An older Temple member who confirmed her unease at the uneven sidewalks in the area was told to request a handicapped Temple parking space. Letters to the *Westfield Leader* both attacked and defended the project. The board allowed individual objectors to give long speeches, one for 40 minutes.

Only a few people disassociated themselves from the negative comments at the hearings, but those few were significant. One was Warren Hanscom, a neighbor adjacent to the parking lot who testified for the project. He recognized that Broad Street is a busy street, felt that it was good to reduce on-street parking, and saw the value in the Temple's growth and success. He asked for better buffering, which the Temple installed.

The Reverend Dee Dee Turlington of the First Baptist Church (and a Westfield homeowner) praised the Temple for hosting town-wide celebrations that bring the religious community together. She supported the goal of improved safety by reducing walking on uneven sidewalks. A neighbor on Wells Street noted Rabbi Sagal's positive and immediate response to a phone call regarding people parking close to his driveway. Negative comments were made by neighbors complaining about the existing facility — lighting, noise from attendees at civic events, removal of some trees, and drainage. One speaker who did not live near the Temple eventually admitted that her description of Temple events was based entirely on hearsay. Some Zoning Board members noted that the civic events complained of were actually of benefit to the Town, such as parties after events at nearby Washington School. Despite the support, on balance, the public commentary was critical and hurtful.

In December 2003, the Board of Adjustment denied the application by a 4-3 vote (four votes were in favor but five favorable votes were required by law). The denial came despite the Temple's agreement to a reduction in paving, an increase in landscaping, and agreement to limit the number of civic events.

After the fact, many neighbors and local officials said they were aghast at the tenor of the remarks. In contrast to the Christmas pageant episode, however, the local Christian clergy proved to be supportive. They volunteered their help, preached sermons, and wrote letters on Temple Emanu-El's behalf.

Rev. Turlington exemplified this support when she wrote about the lack of civility in the proceedings. While noting that many speakers were entirely appropriate in their remarks, she added, "But a number of speakers, not immediately affected, but projecting in their own minds some change in the community they do not like, were out of line . . . and they used descriptive terms that could not help but offend the members of the Temple." She commended the restraint shown by representatives of Temple Emanu-El and by some adjacent homeowners in the debate, but said, "I call on the rest of us — the average citizens who listened in on this debate — to exercise communal self-discipline in the future. When an individual becomes offensive and disrespectful, the persons attacked should not have to defend themselves; the onlookers should do so first."[6]

After the denial, Temple Emanu-El sought judicial relief. In March 2004, an appeal was filed in the Superior Court of New Jersey maintaining that the plan satisfied all requirements for the variances requested. The appeal also stated that the Zoning Board of Adjustment's variance denial and indeed the Town's underlying zoning requirements violated Temple Emanu-El's civil and First Amendment rights and the Temple's rights and privileges under the Religious Land Use and Institutionalized Persons Act (RLUIPA), a federal statute. Under RLUIPA, a governmental agency, including the Town and its land use boards, cannot act to place a substantial burden on the free exercise of religion, and if they do, they must justify their action as the least re-strictive means needed to accomplish the Town's legitimate goals. Perhaps because the appeal exposed the Town and the board to damages and responsibility for the Temple's counsel fees, they settled the appeal on terms similar to those the board had rejected.

In the spring of 2005, Union County Assignment Judge Walter Barisonek approved the settlement "provided a public meeting was held" so the public could comment on the settlement.[7] The number of spaces, landscaping, drainage, and other terms of the settlement were explained in detail, including some constructive modifications requested by the Town itself (which had not been involved in the Board of Adjustment hearings). There were two more public meetings, this time with five-minute limitations on each speaker. Even though some neighbors were still unhappy, the Board of Adjustment voted unanimously to approve the parking lot. Nearly two and a half years had elapsed since the filing of the initial application.

Despite the length of the process, the parking lot experience was in some significant ways a better one than the pageant litigation more than 30 years earlier. The project design was changed to reflect public comment. The number of spaces was reduced, landscaping was enhanced (including at the boundary with Mr. Hanscom to the west and along Broad Street), and lighting was modified to reduce off-site impact. Some spaces were even converted to grass over masonry pavers and are roped off except during the High Holy Days. Safety of traffic circulation through the Temple property was very much improved, resulting in the present one-way flow; the dedicated left and right turns at the exit driveway reduce backups on Broad Street and in the parking lot at busy times. The Town adopted an ordinance prohibiting cars from parking or "standing" in front of the Temple, further enhancing traffic flow.

Neighbors had complained about people talking or smoking behind the Temple late at night; this is no longer allowed. Shades were placed at second floor windows at the new Kroloff Center for Jewish Learning. The kitchen doors remain closed when the kitchen is in use. The number of civic events at the Temple is limited to 12, which the Temple deemed sufficient, and they must end by midnight.

All of the changes were facilitated by the Temple's willingness to stand up to the negative comments and bigotry it faced, as difficult as that was, and use the legal process available to it as well as the positive support of community clergy and some neighbors. Through that process, the Temple could accommodate neighbors' legitimate concerns and provide a safer facility and neighborhood. Ultimately the parking lot experience was a triumph for the rule of law and, therefore, for everyone.

Postscript: The parking lot experience is not atypical of development applications for religious institutions, often regional in nature, always tax-exempt, and not viewed as job generators, especially if the house of worship is not "mainstream." The process can often be as difficult as the Temple experienced. In some communities, the spirit of compromise and appreciation of the value of diversity never develops. That was not true here. The resolution of the Temple parking lot episode suggests that in the end, Westfield was able to reject bigotry and emerge stronger than before.

Commentary

Rabbi Douglas Sagal
Temple Emanu-El Senior Rabbi

I THINK IT IS SAFE TO SAY THAT THE RELATIONSHIP OF TEMPLE EMANU-EL TO THE larger community is both positive and strong. Many good-hearted people in the community were shocked by the ugliness of the parking lot campaign, and a certain atmosphere of good will emerged in the wake of that process, a good will that continues to this day. In recent years, we have seen nationally the re-emergence of racism, prejudice, intolerance, and contempt for certain religions, particularly Islam. For too many years those of us who occupy pulpits have been silent in the face of a growing ugliness in our national discourse. I do believe that we are challenged now to confront the xenophobia of modern-day America and called back to striving for the great ideal that is America.

Chapter Notes

1. Evelyn Averick, *A Historic Narrative: The Story of Temple Emanu-El, Westfield, New Jersey. In Honor of the 30th Anniversary, 1950-1980* (May 1981), 16.

2. Averick, *Historic Narrative,* 20.

3. *Westfield Leader,* Jan. 18, 1973, 1.

4. Ibid,. Feb. 15, 1973, 1.

5. Ibid,, Feb. 13, 2003, 5.

6. Ibid., Jan. 22, 2004, 7.

7. Ibid., April 28, 2005, 2.

PART II

In the Congregation

LEARN. PRAY. DO JUSTLY.

CHAPTER THREE

"Praised Be God Now and Forever": A Reflection on Sixty Years of Prayer and Three Prayer Books

Rabbi Mary L. Zamore

Jewish Center of Northwest New Jersey, Washington, New Jersey

Temple Emanu-El Student/Assistant/Associate Rabbi, 1996–2002

PRAYER FOR THE REFORM MOVEMENT IS A PARADOX, AS WE STRIVE TO INNOVATE prayer, yet preserve its core. Rooted in the reform of both liturgical substance and style, our branch of Judaism has had several "official" prayer books over its 150-year history, from Rabbi Isaac Mayer Wise's *Minhag America* (1857) to our present-day *Mishkan Tefilah* (2006). In its 60 years as a prayer community, Temple Emanu-El has known three official Reform Movement prayer books — the *Union Prayer Book* (UPB), *Gates of Prayer*, and *Mishkan Tefilah*, each reflecting an era in our synagogue's life.

Change and Transition

IN SOME WAYS, THE CHICKEN AND EGG QUESTION APPLIES TO PRAYER BOOK REFORM. We can ask, "Has the Reform Movement produced new prayer books in response to a changing world, or does a new prayer book change the community that engages it?" The answer can be seen as both. As we examine the three prayer books used by Temple Emanu-El, we will explore the generations these liturgies sought to address and the catalyst of change the books became within our community.

Temple Emanu-El was founded to bring together Jews of different identities: Reform, Conservative, and Orthodox. However, the founders agreed that a Reform affiliation with some traditional elements would serve their community best. The synagogue's first rabbi, Ezra Spicehandler, skillfully crafted a compromise designed to bring the diverse community together. *Kipot* were worn on the *bimah* but not required for the congregation. Holidays were observed for two days and Hebrew was more prominent in the service than at other Reform-affiliated congregations.

The history of the UPB started well before the founding of Temple Emanu-El. The 1892 version was intended to be an outgrowth of *Minhag America*, which provided English translations of the Hebrew prayers while providing a shortened version of the traditional liturgy. Isaac Mayer Wise's prayer book also dropped references to a personal Messiah as well as calls for the restoration of the Davidic dynasty.

This was the beginnings of Reform Judaism. American Jews were focused on assimilating, on being integrated into the universities and workplaces. Reform Judaism allowed modern Jews to retain their Jewish identities while balancing them with their secular learning and secular aspirations. As for the prayer services, there was a conscious effort to mimic Protestant church services with their decorum, neat pews, hymns, and organ music.[1]

Of course, there was always disagreement within our movement as to how much modern Jews should shed their traditional identities. Isaac Mayer Wise was a proponent of moderate change, but others wanted more assimilation. By the time the Central Conference of American Rabbis (CCAR) released the UPB in 1892, a modern, radically Reform wing led by Rabbi David Einhorn had gathered enough backing to force the CCAR to recall the UPB and replace it with the 1895 version, which reflected the tenets of what we now call Classical Reform Judaism. This UPB "rejected traditional Jewish tenets such as peoplehood, chosenness, a personal Messiah, resurrection, and a return to the Land of Israel. It also deleted the *musaf* ('additional' Shabbat service) as well as any references to the priesthood and the sacrificial cult, which [were] deemed to be nonrational and unimportant to modern Judaism."[2] The prayer book also emphasized decorum by eliminating most opportunities for congregational participation. Instead, the rabbi, called minister, and a trained choir led the prayers. Instructions for standing and sitting were provided.

There were two more editions of the UPB (1922 and 1941). The prayer leader was relabeled as "rabbi." By 1937, the CCAR passed the first Reform platform supporting the rebuilding of Palestine. The 1941 edition, which Temple Emanu-El adopted in 1950, reflected this sense of peoplehood.

By the 1960s the UPB was dated. That decade's cultural revolution with its emphasis on informality and ethnic pride had touched Reform Judaism as much as any other part of American society. Reform Jews were praying with more Hebrew, had a strong interest in the Shoah and Zionism, were embracing Jewish pride in reaction to the Six-Day War, were gathering to save Soviet Jewry, and were proud to be Jews. The style of prayer in congregations was deeply influenced by the highly participatory and emotive style innovated in the Reform Jewish youth camping movement. The Reform Movement needed a prayer book to reflect this new generation.

Edited by Rabbi Chaim Stern and overseen by a committee chaired by Rabbi Stanley Dreyfus, *Gates of Prayer* made its debut in 1975. At 779 pages, it provides many alternative versions of services, including 10 for Friday night worship. Each service reflects a particular theology or demographic found within the Reform Movement. Thus one *Gates of Prayer* service de-emphasizes the deistic view of God, while another is more traditional with expanded Hebrew and literal translations. Reflecting the suburban baby boom and its child-centric generation, there are two different children's services, one for young children and another for older ones. *Gates of Prayer* includes a Holocaust commemoration and an Israeli Independence Day celebration. Satisfying the growing Reform thirst for poetic prayer and a wide range of musical genres, *Gates of Prayer* is filled with many additional readings and song texts. It not only offered much more Hebrew but it was also the first Reform prayer book to be offered with an optional opening from the right or the left. The tone throughout is participatory and contemporary, moving away from the formality of the UPB.

The 2006 *Mishkan Tefilah* sought to fix *Gates of Prayer*'s deficits and address the newest generation of Reform Jews. The new prayer book was produced in several stages, beginning in 1985. While *Gates of Prayer* was beloved, there was a concern that it did not provide a cohesive liturgy. The book also used masculine language, which did not reflect our egalitarian ideology. The first woman rabbi, Sally Preisand, was ordained in 1972, but there were few women rabbis, rabbinic students, or even lay leaders for years to come. The first woman cantor, Barbara Ostfeld-Horowitz, was invested in 1975. *Gates of Prayer* had missed the call for gender-neutral language by just a few years.

As HUC-JIR professor Rabbi Lawrence Hoffman wrote in his monograph analyzing the newest prayer needs of the Reform community, "We are a generation who values personalism over peoplehood; we are engaged in individual searches for the sacred; we are a diverse group of constituencies within one community; there is a growing interest in the choreography of prayer, ritual, and feminism." Hoffman also emphasized that the laity wanted to be part of the creation of the new prayer book.[3] *Mishkan Tefilah* was designed to address this latest generation of Reform Jews and their needs.

Avoiding Growing Pains

REFORM JUDAISM IS A "CONGREGATIONIST" RELIGION, MEANING THAT WE GATHER in independently governed groups at the congregational level. While we self-affiliate with the Reform Movement, no one central authoritative person or body dictates what prayer book we must use. Therefore, our choice of liturgy is our own, steered by the partnership between clergy and lay leaders. Temple Emanu-El's decision to adopt a new prayer book was an important choice not taken lightly. On the practical side, it was a serious economic commitment to change prayer books, especially when the congregation is the largest in New Jersey. Even more importantly, it was an emotionally weighty decision. A new prayer book is adopted only when the benefits far outstrip the growing pains. Our familiarity with our prayer book is an emotional bond; it is a safe connection. To ruffle that bond requires communal support and an artfully led transition.

Old familiar prayers can function as a mantra. Sure of the prayer order and page numbers, we pray on autopilot and relax as if with an old friend. A new prayer book with its new format and readings wakes us up, taking us out of the meditative state into a very rational, conscious place. While it can be unsettling, this disruption can bring new focus to our prayers. Balance is found as we become familiar with the new.

Change: A Personal View

WHILE I GREW UP USING THE UPB IN EARLY CHILDHOOD, I REALLY KNOW *Gates of Prayer* as THE prayer book. I know how to sing *Aleinu* in English and "God of Might," but my heart is with the book from which I prepared to become a bat mitzvah, a confirmand, and a rabbi. The readings and page numbers are familiar friends, comfortable and easy-going. When I pray from *Gates of Prayer*, I pray a mantra of Hebrew and English and find that different words and phrases jump out at me as needed. Sometimes it seems like those readings and prayers can speak to me as if they knew the inner challenges and triumphs of my life.

I wrote my undergraduate thesis on the movement towards a new prayer book, examining the innovative ways individual Reform prayer communities updated *Gates of Prayer*, while still using the basic structure of the prayer book. Technology allowed the more frequent change of liturgy. If one wanted to use a set of special readings and songs to complement a particular theme, it was easy to paste it up and, at first mimeograph, and then later photocopy it. Handout sheets and homemade handout prayer books became a regular part of Reform Judaism. Computer programs developed to facilitate the creation of these supplementary services. I did a lot of cutting and pasting when I served as a rabbi at Temple Emanu-El. I created youth services, celebratory services, Tisha B'Av services, and many, many handouts to enrich Friday night services. However, in all these cases, *Gates of Prayer* and its approach to prayer was the backbone of the service.

Some of these supplements to *Gates of Prayer* were to compensate for its deficits. Since *Gates of Prayer* was not written with gender-neutral language, prayer leaders were left with the choice of reading prayers as is, or verbally changing the language as one read the prayers. Of course, this only applied to the English translations and readings. Many congregations were changing the prayers to reflect the completely egalitarian nature of Reform Judaism. At Temple Emanu-El, it was our *minhag* (custom) for the prayer leader to change the masculine God language, but to encourage the congregation to read what was written. We felt it was too confusing otherwise, since the changes could greatly alter the grammar of the sentences. Often, individuals would also change the God language, and we would end up with a cacophony. How un-Reform!

Gender-neutral language was not the only thing lacking. Reform Jews use modern poetry as an extension and sometimes a substitution for the normative rubrics of prayer. Lovers of innovative prayer, we crave new readings and songs. We used supplementary handouts to provide more contemporary voices, especially those of Israeli poets, women, and modern Jewish American writers.

A successor to *Gates of Prayer* was long in the making. When I completed my thesis in 1991, leaders of the Reform Movement anticipated a new prayer book within five to eight years. In reality, it took a full 15 years.

During my years as a rabbi at Temple Emanu-El, we had the opportunity to pilot drafts of *Mishkan Tefilah*. A prominent congregation in the Reform Movement, Temple Emanu-El has always been eager to lead and influence the greater movement. As a young rabbi, I especially took notice of the way Rabbi Kroloff prepared the congregation to transition to the new prayer book. He knew that piloting the drafts was an important step in acclimating the congregation to the idea of a new prayer book. As a member of *Mishkan Tefilah*'s editorial committee, he also knew that the congregation's feedback would help shape its final version. The ritual committee was especially supportive and involved in this process. Transparency and public discourse were important to the adoption of *Mishkan Tefilah*.

When the pilot galleys arrived, we took great care to prepare the service. This prayer book offered a very different format from that of *Gates of Prayer*, with several versions of a prayer on each page. We had to provide very clear instructions as to where we were on the page in order to keep everyone together as we explored this new way of praying. Although we recognized that frequent verbal directions disrupted the flow of prayer and did not raise the expectation of prayer book literacy, it was necessary. Using the draft was important, but also a very self-conscious experience. We were all thinking about the prayers as we prayed. Each time we piloted the draft, Rabbi Kroloff facilitated feedback discussions after services and convened extra meetings of the ritual committee. Overall, the reactions we conveyed to the CCAR were strong — both in favor of and opposed to what was on the page.

Today, *Mishkan Tefilah* is a regular part of our prayer landscape. The page feels familiar, and I know almost all the page numbers. When I think about the flow and theme I want for a service, I can easily access what I want from the wide variety of readings and songs in the service. Of course, there always seems to be something else we need. During my eight years at Temple B'nai Or in Morristown, we frequently had a Shabbat handout to provide supplementary prayers and especially music. I guess we would not be Reform Jews without that impulse to keep changing.

At a recent CCAR convention I experienced *Visual Tefilah*, a new way to pray produced by the CCAR and based on *Mishkan Tefilah*. Rather than holding a prayer book, worshippers see the prayers projected onto large screens in front of the entire congregation. I have to admit it did not feel like my cup of tea. I felt bare without holding a book in my hands. My body even felt strange without my neck arched over a prayer book. I missed the intimacy between me and the prayers. At times I was distracted by the graphics accompanying the prayers. With "*Ma Tovu*, How goodly are your tents O Jacob," the slide showed a tent. I started to daydream about all the different types of tents that could have been portrayed and wondered if the image limited the imagination. Every time I felt hypercritical, I tried to remember how I felt when I encountered other new forms of prayer.

I recently participated in a daylong CCAR presentation on *Visual Tefilah*, which included extensive training on how to use this new technology. I am starting to warm up to it. Many of the other rabbis at the program were already using it, and I was surprised to learn how readily their congregations have adopted it. After hearing their enthusiastic reports, I am particularly interested in how to apply this new technology to settings like religious school, learners' services, special services, and prayers during dinners. The ability to focus everyone's attention to the screen and move as slowly or quickly as needed would be fantastic for teaching. Children in particular can get distracted by holding the prayer book and by its busy pages. And in this age of green practices, it would be great to be able to offer special readings without having to create many one-time-use handouts.

In the training, Rabbi Dan Medwin demonstrated using an iPad with a remote and a projector so that one rabbi can control the whole thing. I felt a little out of it since I did not even own a smartphone (yet). He talked about the fact that younger adults feel so comfortable with technology that this will surely be the wave of the future. It struck me that one of *Mishkan Tefilah*'s strengths is that it has so many options on one page. As the congregation prays, one can wander away mentally to explore a commentary on the prayers and then return as wanted. With one big screen, there is only one option. It seems paradoxical for the "I" generation to have so few options. Maybe the next wave will be an app on our mobile devices that hooks us into the prayer service when we enter the sanctuary but allows us to explore other prayers, readings, and commentaries on our own. Maybe when we celebrate Temple Emanu-El's next landmark anniversary, ushers will be handing out iPads instead of prayer books.

Chapter Notes

1. Michael A. Meyer, PhD, *Response to Modernity: A History of the Reform Movement in Judaism* (New York: Oxford University Press, 1988), 241.

2. Elliot L. Stevens, "The Prayer Books, They Are A'Changin'," *Reform Judaism Magazine*, Summer 2006. http://reformjudaismmag.org/Articles/index.cfm?id=1150

3. Ibid.

CHAPTER FOUR

Jewish Music: From the *Chazzanut* of Vienna to "Fiddler" and Shabbat Hallelu

This chapter begins with Temple Emanu-El Senior Cantor Martha Novick's personal journey through the development of cantorial music, followed by recollections of earlier days by Cantor Emeritus Don Decker and a vision of the future by HUC-JIR Professor and Cantor Benjie Ellen Schiller.

Transforming the Music of the Synagogue

Cantor Martha Novick
Temple Emanu-El Senior Cantor

RECENTLY, I WAS LOOKING THROUGH MY MUSIC LIBRARY, SEARCHING FOR something special to sing at a Shabbat service. As I looked at some pieces, I realized it had been many years since I have seen or even considered using any of them. A feeling of sadness came over me. I didn't feel nostalgia but true sadness. I have, for the most part, abandoned that style of liturgical music.

How could this have happened? After all, I am the cantor of this congregation and all musical decisions are part of my responsibility. I spent four years as a cantorial student learning about this music with the understanding that this was the face of Reform Jewish music. What happened to the oath I took upon investiture that I would uphold this tradition and serve my congregation with a full heart?

The answer is complicated, but it does reflect the changing world, both Jewish and musical, in which we live.

I grew up in a liberal Conservative congregation, Oheb Shalom in South Orange, New Jersey. The beauty of the service had to do with its inherent dignity. We had an organ and a choir, and the officers of the congregation were on the *bimah* every Shabbat morning wearing hats. The congregation had an intense love of the music of the service. The cantor, Dr. Edgar Mills, who grew up in Austria, had a truly great voice. He understood the impact of music on a service and always included congregants. The music was majestic yet sweet. It was beautiful and enriching, yet we were part of it.

When I came to Temple Emanu-El more than 25 years ago, the musical culture was as it had been in Reform Judaism for close to a hundred years. Cantor Decker sang the song of Reform Judaism to the highest degree. He is a talented musician and a fine composer; his arrangement of "*Shalom Rav*" is still sung on *Kol Nidre*. Cantor Decker's musical choices reflected the time and culture of Reform worship and the dignity of our musical heritage. He made music an important part of the synagogue and the service, and he created our Temple choir, which remains an integral part of our worship service on Shabbat and during the High Holy Days.

I was poised to continue using the same style of music because in 1986 I had no reason to question our tradition. But, as Cantor Decker knew, it is never about the cantor but about how the congregation perceives and responds to the music. The ideals of HUC-JIR, the cantorial school where I was trained, and the cantor I ultimately became seem like two completely different professions. Accepting change is difficult, but had I remained in this traditional genre, I would have been out.

So what changed? The musical world . . . Reform Judaism . . . Temple Emanu-El . . . me.

One of those life-changing moments was Rabbi Marc Disick's installation as assistant rabbi in 1986, the year I came to Emanu-El. Steve Dropkin, who grew up at Temple Emanu-El, and Cantor Susan Caro sang and played guitar for the event. Now, I grew up with folk music and Peter, Paul & Mary, but guitars in synagogue? At that time guitar or "camp music," as it was known, was looked down upon. But when I heard Susan and Steve rehearsing, I was moved by the beauty and simplicity of their style, so much so that I arranged for them to return twice a year for a "folk music" Shabbat. I began to think there was a place for it, yes, in synagogue. The music's engaging qualities were incorporated more and more into the service. This change was very much in keeping with what was beginning to happen in the larger world of religious music.

At a Biennial several years ago, URJ President Rabbi Eric Yoffie challenged Reform congregations to explore new ways to bring more people to Shabbat services. I realized that congregants value two things in a service — a good sermon and inviting music — and that music could play a very important role in meeting this challenge. Rabbi Yoffie's Biennial address made me think outside the box. With the blessing of Rabbi Kroloff, Shabbat Hallelu was born. Shabbat Hallelu, a high-energy, lively music service, was really the turning point. At first we were apprehensive. Would older people require an alternative service, closer to what they were used to? We needn't have worried. It was a miracle! People of all ages showed up, sang, even danced in the aisles. It brought young and old together and touched everyone's soul. Who said services can't be joyful and uplifting? People were able to express themselves in worship in ways they never dreamed possible.

Looking back, I realize that whatever is happening here at Emanu-El has been ahead of the curve in Reform Jewish music, at least regarding worship. We were among the first to institute this innovation, and it quickly became part of the culture of the congregation. Shabbat Hallelu, held the first Friday night of every month, is now in its twelfth year and more popular than ever, often attracting as many as five hundred people.

Like ours, many Reform congregations are conflicted about the use of the organ. Originating in German Reform Jewish practice, when Jewish worship sought to emulate church services and move away from the *shtetl*, organ music is still identified with American Reform Judaism. While contemporary Jewish music is moving toward piano, keyboard, and guitar, some still enjoy the organ and want it to remain a part of worship.

We resolved this issue by using organ music on the second Shabbat of the month, when the choir sings. Their repertoire derives primarily from nineteenth- and twentieth-century Jewish music, and they enjoy having organ accompaniment. I play keyboard when we incorporate newer repertoire. The choir is happy to include a range of styles, also singing familiar congregational melodies specially arranged for choirs. In this way we preserve the older melodies people know and at the same time engage the congregation in singing, enhanced by a beautiful choral arrangement.

On the third Friday night of the month, Zimrat Shabbat, the music tends to be more contemplative and meditative. We use familiar Kabbalat Shabbat melodies and reinvigorate them with guitar and percussion. People of all ages enjoy it, especially families celebrating their b'nei mitzvah.

We use a more Chasidic style with *niggunim* (Chasidic chants and melodies) and stories on the fourth Friday night. The music is mostly *a capella* with some keyboard accompaniment, but we generally rely on our own lively spirit to accompany us through the service. This is in keeping with renewed interest in the Chasidic musical tradition throughout the Jewish world.

Coming full circle, the URJ 2011 Biennial service, which Rabbi Sagal, Rabbi Kroloff, and I were privileged to conduct in honor of Rabbi Yoffie, was thrilling. It was an awesome and sometimes daunting challenge to meet the spiritual needs of six thousand worshippers all in one room! Once again, we were inspired to bring the best of the world of Jewish music to Temple Emanu-El and, this time, the best of Temple Emanu-El to the Reform Jewish world.

Choral Works, Concerts, and Musicals

Cantor Emeritus Don Decker, 1960–86
Temple Emanu-El

T HE MUSIC DURING MY YEARS AT TEMPLE EMANU-EL CONSISTED OF THE traditional chants of Salomon Sulzer and Louis Lewandowski and other congregational chants still in use at most Reform congregations today. In order to encourage more congregational input, simple melodic songs of inspiration were introduced, such as those of Debbie Friedman.

Special concerts and musicals were part of many enrichment programs. "Anatevka" (similar to music in *Fiddler on the Roof*) was brought to us by Evelyn Averick and performed by congregants, followed by *Victory at Masada*, composed by Martin Kalmanoff and directed by Jack Rocket. *Milk and Honey* by Jerry Herman was directed by Marcy Decker, who was in the original Broadway production. "Mostly Mozart" concerts, managed by Claire Angel, and a violin concert by Itzhak Perlman were highlights.

We had many fine organist–choir directors and choirs of professional singers and congregants. One of our organists, Joseph Colaneri, is now on the roster of conductors at the Metropolitan Opera Company. Choral works by cantors who composed temple music, as well as complete services, were commissioned and introduced for the first time at Temple Emanu-El.

Postscript: Temple Emanu-El also welcomed an extraordinary roster of *Kol Nidre* instrumental soloists in the early years, including Jascha Silberstein, principal cellist for the Metropolitan Opera Company, and Lorne Munroe, principal cellist first for the Philadelphia Orchestra, then for the New York Philharmonic.

Jill Spasser, a member of Temple Emanu-El who went on to become a cantor and faculty member at the HUC-JIR (now Debbie Friedman) School of Sacred Music, led the choir as a volunteer for more than 10 years.

Visioning the Future:
"A Loving, Spiritual Presence"

Cantor Benjie Ellen Schiller

Professor, Cantorial Arts, HUC-JIR Debbie Friedman School of Sacred Music

Cantor, Bet Am Shalom, White Plains, New York

OUR GOAL AS CANTORS IS TO ENGAGE THE CONGREGATION AND OFFER THEM A WAY into Jewish life through music. Cantor Novick, and Cantor Decker before her, are role models for this engagement.

So many today are seeking meaning and spiritual presence. We can draw people in through music, our own Jewish passion, and our loving presence. These are some of the qualities we look for in cantors today.

As Cantor Novick makes clear, much has changed since we were invested. In fact, as of 2012, graduates are no longer "invested" but ordained. We train cantors for five years, helping them learn to partner with rabbis, serving as co-clergy. They are expected to be able to teach and mentor adults, lead prayer, counsel congregants, and so much more.

Today's curriculum for rabbis, cantors, educators, and other students is designed to be intellectual, academic, and practical, but also religious and spiritual. We are challenging this new generation of clergy to experience and develop their own spirituality, asking the kinds of questions for themselves that they will hear from congregants. One of the most popular electives offered to all HUC-JIR students is Spiritual Direction, taught by the Institute of Jewish Spirituality.

We connect with people so briefly that what we give them must be authentic. Music is, in the deepest sense, about spirituality, about giving people meaning. That's the demand on all of us in religious life today.

Musical performance will always be important, but we've added another layer of study we consider just as critical — how to make the music dynamic, relevant, and meaningful to the congregation. We want to synthesize contemporary music with classical styles. As Cantor Novick tells us through her own journey, "folk music" is no longer seen as a "threat," but as part of our musical and spiritual language. I attribute that in part to the involvement of the late Debbie Friedman, for whom the School of Sacred Music has now been renamed. Her personal skills, insightful wit, and creativity made this music relevant and engaging for everyone. She even taught rabbis and cantors how to begin to compose music of prayer for themselves.

Looking to the future, I also see greater specialization. Not everyone will go into congregational work. One of our students, for example, wants to use her music in the service of pastoral care for the ill and elderly. Others will specialize in Jewish education, organizational work, or chaplaincy. Some will explore composition, choral conducting, or concert work. Others will continue their studies in academic or administrative areas.

As Cantor Novick articulates, the challenge is how to broaden our musical style to reach people without watering down the tradition. We do not want to lose our connection to the traditions of our people throughout the world, from Ashkenazic and Sephardic Jewish culture, from ancient times through the Middle Ages to the Reform cantorial traditions of a hundred years ago, to the music and culture of Israel. It is all part of our precious tradition. It is who we are.

The Debbie Friedman School of Sacred Music is responding to what congregations now and in the future are looking for in a cantor: a broad mix of knowledge, skills, interests, and attributes. In terms of music, they want cantors to be able to express and teach a range of styles, from classical to folk, traditional cantorial chant to *niggunim*. Cantors today must be able to go from style to style, collaborate with the rabbi(s) and congregants, involve a choir, and know how to listen to, engage, and empower the congregation. A congregation wants musical and vocal artistry, not just a beautiful voice. They're looking for spiritual presence, dynamism, sensitivity, openness, leadership, a passion for Judaism, and, above all, a loving, spiritual presence.

It's a tall order, but not so very different from what Cantor Novick does every day at Temple Emanu-El.

CHAPTER FIVE

The Changing Profile of the Reform Rabbi

Rabbi Ellen Lewis

Rabbi Emerita, Jewish Center of Northwest New Jersey, Washington, New Jersey
Temple Emanu-El Graduate

Rabbi Jill Maderer

Associate Rabbi, Congregation Rodeph Shalom, Philadelphia, Pennsylvania
Temple Emanu-El Graduate

Rabbi Jeffrey Weill

Rabbi, Ezra Habonim, Niles Township Jewish Congregation, Skokie, Illinois
Temple Emanu-El Graduate / Student Rabbi, 2004–05

With comments by Rabbi Shirley Idelson

Dean, New York School, HUC-JIR

OVER THE PAST 60 YEARS, THE ROLE OF THE RABBI HAS CHANGED SIGNIFICANTLY IN some ways and remained constant in others. This chapter provides an overview from the standpoint of different generations: Rabbi Ellen Lewis, ordained in 1980, Rabbi Jill Maderer, in 2001, and Rabbi Jeffrey Weill, launching his second career, in 2007. Rabbi Shirley Idelson, Dean of the New York School, HUC-JIR, the Reform Jewish rabbinical school, gives her perspective on the core values of rabbinic education, what congregations seek in a rabbi, and what lies ahead.

The Ideal Rabbi through the Decades: Priest, Prophet, Teacher

THE CENTRAL ASPECT OF THE RABBI'S MISSION, "TO HELP US EXPERIENCE GOD'S presence in the world, especially when people are in need," is unchanging, according to Rabbi Idelson. Just as in ancient times, rabbis mine the tradition and wrestle critically with text to derive contemporary meaning.

One of the areas of change, however, is how people describe "spiritual experience." In the 1940s, it may have meant listening to preachers like Rabbi Stephen S. Wise, founder of the Jewish Institute of Religion and Stephen Wise Free Synagogue, galvanize packed houses with his fiery sermons. Today, while good preaching continues to be highly valued, many are also seeking spirituality in prayer and meditation.

Rabbi Lewis traces the changing emphasis on priest, prophet, and teacher over the years, while Rabbi Maderer speaks to the ongoing challenge to "connect people to Jewish life." The contemporary emphasis on pastoral work reflects a personal search for meaning in today's world.

Rabbinic training has changed with the times. According to Rabbi Idelson, the goal of the school is to provide students with a well of learning and liturgical tradition from which they can draw for the rest of their lives. While traditional rabbinic studies are still primary, today's curriculum features a greater emphasis on pastoral care, clinical counseling, youth work, interfaith outreach, and such supplemental but increasingly necessary skills as human resources, budgeting, fund-raising, and management.

Technology is another factor changing the face of rabbinic education, literally in some instances. Students all over the country, indeed, the world, interact with faculty in virtual classrooms. The school's Jewish studies portal makes a broad range of text instantly available. The vast reservoirs of knowledge available through technology are replacing people who once served as the repositories of tradition. Nonetheless, as Rabbi Idelson notes, "Google can tell you about Shabbat rituals, but it can't make them meaningful. Our rabbis, cantors, and educators are less often called on to be the sources of information, freeing them to be shapers of meaning."

Rabbi Lewis and Rabbi Maderer expand on the themes of rabbinic roles through the decades.

Rabbi Lewis: Rabbis throughout our tradition have combined the roles of priest, prophet, and teacher, with different emphases in each era.

Rabbis of the 1950s emphasized the priestly role. The *bimah* was elevated. Sermons, a critical aspect of rabbinic reputations, were dramatic performances and "reviewed" like Broadway shows. Relationships centered around the sanctuary. Rabbis received greater honor, or *k'vod*, and had more control; there was no need for a "ritual committee" in that era.

While true for many American Classical Reform congregations and their rabbis, this model was less descriptive of Temple Emanu-El. An amalgam of Conservative and Reform, Emanu-El was more traditional in its beginnings. Men wore *kipot* and *tallitot*. The congregation observed two days of Rosh Hashanah, an ongoing tradition. We were fortunate to have Rabbi Jack Stern Jr. as our spiritual leader, a kind and loving man who truly did combine the roles of priest, prophet, and teacher.

In the 1960s, the civil rights era called for a more prophetic rabbinate. Many Reform rabbis assumed leadership roles in the fight for equal rights, taking to the streets in solidarity with the Reverend Dr. Martin Luther King Jr. and others. Temple Emanu-El was a pioneer in social justice early in its history, thanks to strong lay and rabbinic leadership continuing into the present.

Today the roles of teacher, pastor, and counselor are primary. Many women rabbis find this gives them more options than in the past when career ladders were more rigidly defined. Both men and women can be chaplains, education directors, Hillel, organizational, or congregational rabbis. They can work part-time or share the pulpit with a spouse, which would have been unthinkable 60 years ago.

These changing trends are exemplified by my own congregation, from which I recently retired. Congregants came to learn and expected my sermons to teach more than preach. My psychoanalytic training also supported the importance of counseling and pastoral work so valued today.

Another change I've observed is the expectation that rabbis work in partnership with the congregation, including on fund-raising and business issues. This may call for changes in the way rabbis are trained, giving them more exposure to the financial realities of congregational life today.

Rabbi Maderer: Much like the tradition's teaching of Rabbi Zusya, who needed to aspire to be not more like Moses but more like Zusya, I believe the ideal changes from rabbi to rabbi, community to community, team to team. What I can say is that the ideal rabbi, in any age, is one who uses his/her God-given gifts to connect people to Jewish life, and one who has the passion and love for the work enough to know that being a rabbi is the best job in the world.

Differing Levels of Observance: Personal vs. Community

Neither Rabbi Weill nor Rabbi Maderer sees differences in levels of observance as an issue. Rabbi Weill sees a rabbi's greater observance as a validation of authenticity and commitment to the tradition, while Rabbi Maderer calls attention to the importance of the synagogue community's continuing self-renewal as it interacts with the larger world.

Rabbi Weill: Congregants are very comfortable with a rabbi who is more observant than they, and I think that's appropriate. A commitment to some traditional observance by a Reform rabbi helps to establish the rabbi's authenticity as a leader, teacher, and representative of an ancient tradition. It also demonstrates that he or she has thought deeply about *halachah* and has made some personal commitments to it. These commitments include *kashrut* and some level of Shabbat observance. I wear *tzitzit*, tucked in, like many Modern Orthodox men, and I enjoy explaining to my congregants that I do it and why. I reference for them the Shema's *Va'Yomer* paragraph, included in *Mishkan Tefilah*, which describes the edifying purpose of the fringes — to keep one always aware of *mitzvot* and to concentrate one's mind on a proper path. Who would argue? In my congregation's Casual Shabbat Minyan, we chant that paragraph every Shabbat. I have at times suggested to some of my congregants a visit to an Orthodox bookstore in order to pick up *tzitzit*. No one has taken me up on the offer.

Rabbi Maderer: In a nonjudgmental progressive setting, differences in rabbinic and congregational observance do not carry much import. The larger issue is the range of observance throughout a community; it's hard to create community if you are not among people whose practice resembles your own. It's also hard to create community if members of that community are not committed to a level of involvement required to enable them to support one another in their lives.

Classical Reform and other styles as a source of inspiration in one's individual life can vary without tremendous impact. However, when we join together in a congregation, ritual styles that reflect the different cultural backdrop of the past will create a community that feels out of date and out of touch for new people who walk in the door. The power of Torah as a living document and Judaism as a dynamic way of life is in the ability to renew. If, in 2073, we continue to be immersed in *minhag* (custom) 2013, we will have lost that dynamism. If, however, we remain in the world, learning the best from the world around us as it relates to Torah and to spiritual quest, we will offer relevance and vision to Jews, non-Jews, and prospective Jews.

Interfaith and Same-Sex Marriage: "It Will Just Be Known As Marriage"

Rabbi Weill and Rabbi Maderer see no opposition among Reform rabbis to officiating at same-sex marriages and less and less for interfaith marriages.

Rabbi Idelson sees both areas as important for rabbinic training. Students are taught the traditions that apply to same-sex and interfaith marriages and work with the Jewish Outreach Institute to gain a clearer understanding of the issues confronting interfaith families.

Rabbi Weill: I do not know any Reform rabbis who would not officiate at the same-sex wedding of two Jews. As for interfaith officiation, the number of Reform rabbis that take a principled stand against it is shrinking. One Reform rabbi commented, "That train has left the station." I believe the rabbinate has led on the same-sex officiation issue, and that congregants have led on the interfaith officiation issue.

Rabbi Maderer: In the future, interfaith and same-sex marriage will just be known as marriage. We will be honored and proud to welcome anyone into our midst who is committed to the future of the Jewish people and who is open to a deep Jewish journey.

Gender Issues: "We Wanted to Be Rabbis, Not Revolutionaries"

The generational differences on gender issues are clear in the responses by Rabbi Lewis, who entered the rabbinate in the heat of the battle for women's liberation, and Rabbi Maderer, for whom a healthy family life for everyone is far more of an issue.

Rabbi Lewis: In the early days, women were considered radical for wanting to be rabbis, but in actuality we were very conservative. We just wanted to be rabbis, not revolutionaries. We wanted to teach Torah. We wanted to be asked to speak on Maimonides, not on what it was like to be a woman rabbi. We wore rabbinic robes like our male colleagues. We were busy focusing on survival in a traditionally male profession.

Even when I had young children, I was determined to do my pulpit rabbinate a full 45 hours a week. I never used family as an excuse for anything. I did what I needed to do to feel comfortable as a mother without announcing it. I used to call my kids' coaches a year in advance to find out what days they would be playing games. Then I scheduled b'nei mitzvah rehearsals around that schedule. I never missed a game. And I never missed an appointment with a congregant.

Later women rabbis were able to break the mold. Part of the broader women's liberation movement, they were influential in removing gender from the language of prayer. They also had more options for part-time work when children were young and did not have to take full-time pulpits in order to be taken seriously as rabbis.

In my therapy practice, I've found the gender differences to be substantial, particularly on a subconscious level. In earlier generations, (male) rabbis were seen as God. Naturally, since rabbis were male, that meant God was male. I was tickled the first time a 13-year-old girl said to me, "Rabbi Lewis, did you know when I was little, I thought you were God?"

But gender differences in the rabbinate are complex. People see their rabbis through the eyes of transference, and transference knows no gender. Male rabbis can be seen as mommy and female rabbis as daddy. Still, I think it is more usual for people to have very different unconscious responses to women. At some deep level, they experience what therapists would call a "mother" transference: "You're there for me 24/7.

You love me unconditionally, and your own needs never enter in." This is less true for male rabbis. If people see a male rabbi in the supermarket, for example, they tend to think, "He's such a good guy, helping his wife." If they see a female rabbi with a shopping cart, the response is more likely to be, "Look how she's spending her time. Shouldn't she be in temple?"

Rabbi Maderer: Today we are blessed with opportunity for both men and women. Nonetheless, just as there is overt and subtle sexism in the secular world, it exists too in congregational life. My biggest concern is that our congregational and larger world has not yet created a society that supports families in an ideal way. In the corporate and congregational worlds, parental leave is limited, child care is not abundant, and breast-feeding is not fully supported. Fathers are barely asking for or receiving parental leave when a child is born or adopted.

Perhaps in the next 60 years, we will have learned from other countries and dedicate our own thinking to solutions that support people and families in all of their fullness.

The Role of the Spouse: "A Special Place in Heaven"

All spoke about the complexities of being married to a rabbi. Differing expectations for men and women create further complications, but, as Rabbi Maderer points out, the male spouses of female and gay clergy have helped congregants see them not as "role models" but as part of the community. Rabbi Weill affirms the value of the rabbinic family's Jewish and congregational commitment, regardless of gender.

Rabbi Lewis: Life is especially complex and challenging for spouses of congregational rabbis. Their lives can never be totally separate. It's that much harder if the rabbi is having difficulties because the spouse has no one to talk to. When women started becoming rabbis, no one knew what to expect of the spouse. The key question must then shift from the role of the spouse to how rabbis and lay people can make each other feel valued.

Rabbi Maderer: In the early days, of course, the rabbi's wife was expected to be there at synagogue. She didn't work, she was a stay-at-home mother, and that's not "real" work! Now that, in 2013, some spouses are men, of course we cannot expect the same level of presence. They have "real" jobs! Such absurd assumptions and double standards may have let the first generation of male clergy spouses off the hook. Over the next 60 years, we will eliminate the "hook" itself.

The question of the clergy spouse's role is tied up in gender roles, gender restrictions, and gender expectations. When all clergy were men, female spouses were expected to support the clergy role in public ways. It has taken the presence of male spouses of female clergy or gay clergy to help us all realize that the spouse is a part of the community, not a paid or official role model for Jewish life. Although I think clergy spouses should be restricted from serving in governance of the synagogue, in general, specific expectations are unreasonable. Clergy spouses should be welcomed into a community, respected for their individuality, and given the freedom to find their own way (knowing there is a special place in heaven reserved for them!).

Sixty years from now, there will be no such thing as defining the clergy spouse role.

Rabbi Weill: In the recent past, it seems that a Reform rabbinic spouse who did not have her (usually) own busy professional schedule was considered overly traditional, similar to Hillary Rodham Clinton's quip about staying home and "baking cookies." What self-respecting spouse (especially wife) would want to do such things? My observation, though, is that congregants want to see a spouse who is involved in the congregational community. They yearn to see it, in fact. It reflects on the rabbi's commitment to the congregation and on the Jewish commitment of the rabbinic family. Such involvement need not, and should not, preclude the spouse's own career. All congregants want to see is a spouse who is interested in the welfare of the congregation and who is happy to be involved.

Drawing Boundaries: "Strong but Permeable"

Rabbi Lewis and Rabbi Maderer note the challenges but emphasize the value of the rabbinic-congregational relationship, good communication, and a shared focus on Jewish growth.

Rabbi Lewis: We had ground rules that made for an organic, harmonious relationship. The congregation was very protective of me, and I never "counted hours." My congregational friendships were all within the context of temple life; very few congregants had my cell phone number or personal email.

You can't expect the congregation to take care of you; you have to take care of yourself. You can't expect the congregation to take care of your family; that is your job. When I first entered HUC, Rabbi Kroloff told me it was important to learn how to say no. I don't think I understood at the time how important that skill is. But you also have to know how to say yes at the right times.

The issue of personal boundaries is never resolved once and for all. It is something you have to work on every day. It helps to be in a place where you can communicate with and be understood by your congregants. Once you have a real and deep relationship with a congregation, you can say and do almost anything because the context is love.

Rabbi Maderer: I believe it's important for clergy to protect our lives and families with strong but permeable boundaries. But our greatest concern here is to help facilitate a community that has more interesting things to discuss than its clergy's family. People are so busy, but activity does not always mean productivity, and an over-programmed membership does not always mean a deeply engaged one. When members are devoted to personal and communal Jewish growth, that journey is our focus, and we have little time to violate privacy.

What about the clergy's own time? No clue!

Growing Up at Emanu-El: Personal Recollections

The rabbis remember Temple Emanu-El rabbis as community leaders, teachers, strong advocates for social justice, and inspirations for young people.

Rabbi Lewis: I don't know what the role of the rabbi is at Temple Emanu-El now, but I know how I perceived it as a child growing up. Rabbis at Emanu-El were always respected; there was a great sense of *k'vod harav* (honor to the rabbi). I remember feeling that as a little girl for Rabbi Stern. The rabbis were respected both for their knowledge of Torah and for their participation as community leaders. When there was an issue in my family ("I want to go to the March on Washington, Dad"), my father called the rabbi. When Westfield High School canceled our Moratorium Day in the fall of 1969, I called Rabbi Kroloff and asked if we could bring our speakers to the Temple. He immediately said yes. Our rabbis were always leaders and teachers, not unquestioned authorities but powerful and influential ones.

Rabbi Maderer: Two things stand out. First, the assistant rabbi's leadership of or connection with the youth group, with which I was very involved, made a tremendous impression. Both the rabbis and the non-rabbi youth group leaders made us feel that there was nothing more important in the congregation than us. I'm not sure that the youth world nationally is thriving at the level it did. I believe there is a new URJ effort to support more full-time rabbis and professionals in this work movement-wide. That would be wonderful to see.

Second, a very inspiring component of my upbringing at Temple Emanu-El was Rabbi Kroloff's social justice work. He led with a voice of conscience that is missing from many current models.

Rabbi Weill: Much of what I do as a rabbi I consider through the prism of my experiences both as a kid and as a student rabbi at Temple Emanu-El. I wonder, "What would Rabbi Kroloff do?" or "What would Rabbi Sagal do?"

My sense of the rabbi's role has certainly changed since I became a rabbi. During my childhood and teen years, I expected the rabbi primarily to be a moral force in my life and to be a moral voice in the community. This is what I expected and desired. Rabbi Kroloff certainly fulfilled my expectations beautifully, as did Rabbi Arnie Gluck, the assistant during my formative years in the senior youth group. I did not expect the rabbi to represent the *halachic* tradition. In fact, "*halachah*" likely was not part of my vocabulary. Perhaps because my focus has changed, and perhaps because Reform Judaism has changed, I see myself now more as a teacher in other senses. I want to transmit the thrill I get from Jewish literature, traditional to contemporary. And I want to open my congregants to the possibilities of a little ritual observance in their lives.

Here is what has not changed. Martin Buber's "I-Thou" was and is an influence on Rabbi Kroloff, and I do remember that he faithfully applied that in his relationships with congregants. I have learned this from him. My most important rabbinic role is to see and hear and validate my congregants. And to pray for them too.

Emanu-El graduates who became rabbis, as well as the Temple's senior, associate, assistant, and student rabbis over the past 60 years, exemplify Rabbi Idelson's goals for the rabbis of the future. Drawing on the tradition, they have sought to help people find meaning and experience God's presence in the world from generation to generation.

Commentary

Rabbi Douglas Sagal
Temple Emanu-El Senior Rabbi

As my colleagues have indicated, the role of the rabbi is changing dramatically in our time. The congregational rabbi must be not only a teacher, preacher, and pastor, but also an administrator, CEO, and director of development and marketing. Some of this is inevitable, given the immense changes in our society over the last two decades and the complete and utter triumph of consumerism as the cultural touchstone of our nation. No profession — lawyer, doctor, or accountant — has been unaffected.

The rabbi, however, must remain the premier teacher of Torah for her/his community, the exemplar of Jewish values, and a practitioner of the highest forms of morality. The importance of the rabbi as teacher of Torah and as conveyer of Jewish values can never be compromised. In addition, rabbis must begin to recognize that skilled and knowledgeable lay people can play an important role in both teaching and pastoring the community. We have to be able to expand the term "rabbi" to include, as it were, the many gifted lay people who comprise the Jewish community.

PART III

Meeting
New Challenges

LEARN. PRAY. DO JUSTLY.

CHAPTER SIX

Reform Jewish Outreach: When "Marrying Out" Became "Marrying In"

Rabbi Arnold Gluck

Temple Beth-El, Hillsborough, New Jersey
Temple Emanu-El Student/Associate Rabbi, 1980–86

FOR GENERATIONS, THE JEWISH COMMUNITY'S RESPONSE TO INTERMARRIAGE WAS one-dimensional and negative. Marrying a non-Jew was "marrying out," which was tantamount to opting out of the Jewish community. Against a backdrop of a potent and pervasive anti-Semitism that stigmatized association with Jews, barred Jews from associations, schools, clubs, and many jobs, it was rare for a non-Jew to choose to marry a Jew.

By the 1970s, in the wake of the successes of the civil rights and women's rights movements, it was clear that America was changing. Institutional anti-Semitism virtually disappeared, and Jews became accepted on almost all levels of society. By the mid-'70s intermarriage was becoming a significant phenomenon despite the unyielding disapproval of the American Jewish establishment. In 1977 Rabbi Alexander Schindler, then president of the UAHC, broke with conventional wisdom. He offered a bold new response to intermarriage, launching a program of outreach that welcomed the intermarried into Reform synagogues and encouraged them to make Jewish choices, including raising their children as Jews, and conversion.

This was truly a Big Idea. Why should we assume that Jews who marry non-Jews are marrying out? Why not see it as non-Jews marrying IN? It was not about reorienting Jewish practice to create ecumenism, but rather from the perspective of Jewish particularism, opening the doors of synagogue life to all who would wish to enter. Rabbi Schindler believed with a passion in the power of Judaism to speak to contemporary American life and believed that it could and should compete in the free marketplace of religious ideas that was emerging. He was utterly convinced that Judaism would appeal to the "unchurched," and that many non-Jews were attracted to Jews not in spite of their Jewishness but precisely because of it, drawn to the vibrancy of Jewish life and the warmth of the Jewish family. The Reform emphasis on social justice and community involvement, which characterized synagogues like Temple Emanu-El, he posited, would be attractive to many non-Jews. He was right!

When I came to work at Emanu-El in the summer of 1980, the idea of outreach was in the early stages of implementation, and it captured my imagination. I was fortunate to be at Emanu-El during this period because Rabbi Kroloff, a close confidant of Rabbi Schindler, became an early adopter of this initiative. The UAHC (later URJ) hired Dru Greenwood to be the first outreach coordinator for the New Jersey region, and we worked closely with her in her pioneering role.

Temple Emanu-El was among the first in the nation to offer Introduction to Judaism classes using a new Union curriculum and piloted workshops for intermarried couples and for those considering conversion. The welcome mat was out. We were able to engage with the intermarried to help them make Jewish choices and raise Jewish children. This had a major impact on individual families, who now recognized they were welcome and that there was a place for them in the synagogue.

Temple Emanu-El started performing conversion ceremonies during Shabbat services around this time. The impact of these conversions was significant on Jews and non-Jews alike. Watching people stand up and proclaim their commitment to Judaism inspired some non-Jews who had grown close to Jewish life to ask themselves, "Why not me?" And many Jews who witnessed the same scene were inspired to see being Jewish as a value to be embraced as a choice instead of merely as an accident of birth. This underscored the power of formal conversion for me. If welcoming the intermarried means fudging the boundaries and definitions of Judaism so as to remove all distinctions between Jews and non-Jews, the act of conversion loses its meaning. If anyone can do anything in a Jewish context irrespective of their personal beliefs and faith commitments, what does it mean to be Jewish? It undermines Jewish identity, diminishes the value of Jewish peoplehood, and can have an especially chilling effect on our children's commitment to Judaism.

Formal conversion underscores the importance of *Am Yisrael*, the unique and precious peoplehood of Israel. From its inception this idea was the bedrock on which Temple Emanu-El stood, informing its passionate devotion to the State of Israel and to Jews of other lands, like Ethiopia, Syria, and the Soviet Union. Temple Emanu-El has never, and in my opinion, must never allow its commitment to outreach to weaken our loyalty to Jewish particularism, even as we pursue the universal values of peace, justice, and human dignity.

Maybe the greatest conundrum associated with opening our hearts and our doors to the intermarried is the question of rabbinic officiation at mixed marriages. While some believe it wrong and even hypocritical to refrain from performing the weddings of those we have come to accept and welcome into our congregations, I disagree. It is, in my opinion, legitimate and appropriate to maintain a hierarchy between that which is acceptable and that which we deem to be sacred. And I believe that fidelity to the value of Jewish particularism demands that we not risk forfeiting the ideal of Jewish marriage. I know that others disagree, but I believe that the integrity of Judaism requires this of us, and studies show that the future of the Jewish people in America may depend on it.[1]

Regardless of whether or not a rabbi officiates at mixed marriages, outreach efforts prove effective. Such was the recent finding of a three-year study by The CCAR Task Force on the Challenges of Intermarriage for the Reform Rabbi, chaired by Rabbi Kroloff, and on which Rabbi Mary Zamore and I both served. The experience of the Boston-area Jewish community is particularly instructive in this regard. Thanks to a vibrant partnership between the synagogues and the Jewish Federation, which provided funding for a broad range of outreach programs, the percentage of children of intermarried families being raised as Jews is nearly double the national average, reaching 60 percent. This makes a strong case for the argument that while intermarriage poses challenges for Jewish continuity, there is no inevitable outcome. (*See Rabbi Sagal's discussion of interfaith officiation at Temple Emanu-El followed by discussions of the CCAR's task force report and of two studies on interfaith families in the next chapter.)*

Initiatives like Birthright Israel, which sponsors free trips to Israel for young Jews between the ages of 18 and 26, indicate that it is possible to influence Jewish marriage patterns. Comprehensive studies of Birthright participants reveal a marked decline in their rate of intermarriage compared to the national average. This is a significant phenomenon that will impact the future of American Jewry in positive ways. But given the broader sociocultural context of America today, the rate of intermarriage between Jews and non-Jews is likely to remain high, and we would be well advised to react proactively in the model of the Boston Jewish community.

I believe that people are entitled to marry whomever they want to marry. There is no place for judgment. It is wrong and counterproductive. Our best hope and most constructive policy is to inspire Jewish choices both before and after marriage. Our doors must always be open to interfaith couples, whether or not we perform their weddings, and we should offer a multitude of "yeses" for them. Even under the strictest interpretations of Jewish tradition there are many ways we can embrace and include them and help them to form Jewish families. Personally, I can and want to be their rabbi.

Welcoming interfaith couples into our congregations obligates us to be sensitive and responsive to their special needs. Over the years we have developed programs and workshops to address some of the psychosocial issues that are unique to interfaith families. Judaism gains when interfaith families choose to identify as Jewish, but we must also recognize the loss to the other extended (non-Jewish) family. It is critical to demonstrate care and concern for those families and relationships and to embrace them as well. The Torah's command to "love the stranger" finds expression in this way.

Being inclusive also entails being clear about boundaries and defining the rules for those who want to be part of synagogue life. It is important to do this in order to maintain the integrity both of those who would join us as well as of Judaism. In an atmosphere where conversion is welcomed and encouraged, we need to remember that the non-Jews in our synagogues are "non-Jews by choice." Inviting them to recite prayers or blessings that declare one to be Jewish would be insensitive and inappropriate. Likewise, putting them in a position to make policies about how the

Jewish members of the congregation will fulfill their Jewish obligations would be wrong. This is why my synagogue in Hillsborough has joined many others in producing a document that delineates and defines the boundaries for the participation of non-Jews in the areas of ritual, governance, and membership.

Some interfaith families have chosen to educate their children in more than one religious path. Parents have both the right and the responsibility to decide how to educate their children. But here, too, the synagogue must be thoughtful and clear about its role. As a Jewish institution, its mission is to prepare Jewish children to live Jewishly, not to participate in a tug of war over a child's soul. Consistent with the policy adopted by the URJ, my congregation will not enroll a child in our school who is being formally schooled in another faith. Having clear boundaries provides a place of comfort and confidence for all who wish to join in the fellowship of the community.

We've come a long way from the 1950s when nothing like this was on the radar screen. It has been a seismic shift, both positive and negative. The attitude now is that if you think you shouldn't "marry out," you could be accused of being racist.

We've seen every possible pattern of interfaith relationships, from those in which both partners are actively involved in Jewish life and the children's Jewish identity is clear, to others in which only one partner is involved or neither is. What works? This is a serious question. The percent of children of interfaith marriage being raised as Jews is currently in the mid-20s. Statistics show the third generation virtually drops off a cliff. Can we reverse this trend? Again, the example of Boston tells us that serious outreach efforts can produce extraordinary results.

It's not just interfaith families. Jews with no Jewish education don't present all that differently. For example, a Russian family with a 12-year-old child asked about bar mitzvah. While many might question it, I accepted the family in the spirit of outreach.

This was a lesson I learned at Temple Emanu-El, reinforced by my years in Haifa as part of the Leo Baeck Education Center and rabbi of the progressive Congregation Ohel Avraham, a minority in Israel where Orthodoxy receives official recognition and support. I used the outreach techniques I learned at Emanu-El to reach secular Jews and women there, two sectors who feel alienated from traditional religious institutions.

Some prominent sociologists say the Jewish community has limited resources and should "circle the wagons" by focusing on already committed Jews, supporting day schools, camps, and other Jewish institutions. I disagree. My experience suggests that our outreach efforts benefit those already close to us as well. Outreach classes and programs attract many Jews who are not intermarried, and the emphasis on making Jewish choices inspires the entire Jewish community.

It's not just a question of *who* we will be, but *how*. When we close our doors, it breeds insularity. It changes us. A posture of openness, optimism, and self-confidence produces more positive outcomes than one of defensiveness, pessimism, and fear. If we have something to say to the world, as I believe we do, we should be bold and proclaim it. If we don't have anything to say, that's the *real* crisis.

Chapter Notes

1. According to the National Jewish Population Survey of 2000–01, only a third of the children of intermarriage identify as Jews. "The National Jewish Population Survey 2000–01: Strength, Challenge and Diversity in the American Jewish Population." A United Jewish Communities Report in Cooperation with the Mandell L. Berman Institute – North American Jewish Data Bank, September 2003, updated January 2004. http://www.jewishfederations.org/local_includes/downloads/4606.pdf

CHAPTER SEVEN

Diverse Views on Intermarriage and Outreach

A Letter from Rabbi Sagal

The following letter to the Temple Emanu-El congregation articulates Rabbi Sagal's position on officiating at interfaith marriages.

Rabbi Douglas B. Sagal
November 30, 2011 — *4 Kislev 5772*

Dear members of Temple Emanu-El:

As a rabbi, it is my responsibility to always ponder the future of Temple Emanu-El and to ensure that our future will be bright. It is also my responsibility to work to–wards ensuring the future of the Jewish people as a whole.

One of the great issues that has engaged the Jewish community has been that of interfaith marriage. Over the last several decades, the rate of Jewish men and women falling in love with non-Jewish partners has increased dramatically. Over the summer, I had the opportunity to attend a lecture by Steven Cohen, the preemi–nent researcher on this issue. Among his many conclusions are that intermarriage is an established fact of American Jewish life and that welcoming warmly the 18 to 20 percent of interfaith couples that eventually join congregations is *critical* to the future of the Jewish community.

Rabbinic officiation at interfaith marriages has been a contentious issue. Just as there are people who believe that rabbis *should* officiate at interfaith marriages, there are just as many who are convinced that rabbis should *not* officiate. In my opinion the key question is how we can engage *young people in general* to affiliate with the Jewish community in a meaningful way and raise Jewish families, thus ensuring our future. As I mentioned in my sermon of a year ago, statistics show that it is often *fifteen to twenty years* before the typical Jewish high school graduate affiliates with a synagogue community. The greatest number of young Jews in America are not "reform" or "conservative" or "orthodox" — they are "<u>none of the above</u>."

Given the need to ensure a vibrant Jewish future, and knowing that 18 to 20 percent of intermarried families do affiliate, what can we do to help those young interfaith families who are serious about creating a Jewish home to do so?

It was well over two years ago that the Central Conference of American Rabbis, the umbrella body of Reform rabbis and my own professional organization, decided to study the issue of rabbinic officiation at interfaith marriages. As part of their conclusions, the CCAR has made it clear that the decision to officiate was clearly up to the individual conscience of each rabbi. They also concluded that welcoming interfaith couples with warmth and an open heart was critical to the future of Judaism.

About a year ago, Rabbi Kroloff, our esteemed rabbi emeritus, made the decision, after much reflection, to begin officiating at interfaith marriages under certain conditions. He and I had many lengthy and heartfelt conversations about the issue. He has since officiated at a number of such marriages for couples committed to creating a loving Jewish home together.

I have made the decision to extend the same prerogative to the other ordained clergy on our staff. I make this decision for two reasons.

First, I accord to each clergy member the right to make this decision in keeping with the dictates of their own beliefs and opinions as highly educated members of the rabbinate. This decision is not only in keeping with the priorities of the CCAR, it is, I believe, eminently fair. Second, I truly believe that we as an institution have a loving and sacred obligation to assist couples who wish to make Jewish choices. Temple Emanu-

El can and should remain the spiritual home for those families and their children.

Please note that both Rabbi Erin Glazer and Rabbi Sarah Smiley have indicated that they would be willing to perform interfaith marriages under certain conditions and are ready to begin meeting with potential couples.

In keeping with the CCAR ruling that every rabbi must abide by his or her own conscience, I have decided for the time being to maintain my own position, which is to not officiate. My reasons have much to do with my own understanding and view of the nature of the Jewish wedding and have nothing at all to do with the choice of a Jewish or non-Jewish partner. I have maintained this position for 22 years, even after the bitter sorrow of having to say no to congregants I love, as well as to my own family members. I confess that the hardest thing I have ever had to do is to say no to people that I have watched grow from childhood to adulthood and love like my own. I have agonized and wrestled with this issue for over two decades. Perhaps in years to come, like Rabbi Kroloff, my position will change, but for now, it remains the same. Cantor Novick, after reflection, has also decided to maintain her current policy of refraining from officiation.

As always, I am available to all of you for further discussion and look forward to hearing from you.

It was only a few weeks ago that we read in the Torah of Noah. Noah was, above all else, a builder. A builder of the ark, but also a builder of the Jewish future. Our world is complex and ever-changing, but I am convinced that this decision will help us to create Jewish families and Jewish homes, will strengthen Temple Emanu-El, and will help ensure our Jewish future.

L'shalom,
Rabbi Doug Sagal

The CCAR Task Force Report on Intermarriage

Rabbi Kroloff chaired the CCAR Task Force on the Challenges of Intermarriage for the Reform Rabbi, which issued its report in March 2010. Rabbi Arnold Gluck and Rabbi Mary Zamore, both former Temple Emanu-El rabbis, chaired the research team subcommittee on Engagement and Conversion together with Rabbi Morley Feinstein.

THE TASK FORCE REPORT RECOMMENDS RABBIS CHANGE THEIR PREVIOUS FOCUS from preventing intermarriage, now a given in today's more open society, to engaging intermarried families in Jewish life and living: "In the past, the prevailing view was that intermarriage posed an inevitable loss to the Jewish people and Jewish continuity. Today, we recognize that effective communal outreach makes a difference in bringing intermarried families into our synagogues and Jewish life."

The report recognizes the diversity of opinions and practices regarding rabbinic officiation at interfaith weddings but finds "broad agreement that the most important issue for Jewish continuity is the engagement of intermarried families in meaningful Jewish living." It urges welcoming of intermarried families in congregations and communities and "celebration of their desire to be participating, engaged Jewish households."

Approaches to Jewish learning tailored to interfaith families, programs that integrate them into the congregation, rabbinic counseling and teaching skills that support welcoming, and integration and partnerships with other Jewish organizations that engage the intermarried are strongly encouraged.

The report concludes, "We have learned to look for a future we want to create, not simply an answer or approach to an issue."

A Tale of Two Jewries:
The "Inconvenient Truth" for American Jews

A report by Steven M. Cohen, Research Professor of Jewish Social Policy, Hebrew Union College–Jewish Institute of Religion. The report may be accessed at http://www.jewishlife.org/ publication/a-tale-of-two-jewries/. Copyright © 2006 by Jewish Life Network/Steinhardt Foundation and Steven M. Cohen.

SOCIOLOGIST STEVEN COHEN CITES THE STEEP GENERATIONAL DECLINE IN JEWISH ethnicity, the sense of commitment to Jewish peoplehood, as a key factor in the rise of intermarriage. In his view this rise is "the greatest single threat to Jewish continuity today."

Cohen urges Jewish families and institutions to "increase the cultural, spiritual and social capital of today's Jewish children, so that they will marry Jews and raise their own Jewish children when they mature." He advocates for strengthening Jewish education, camps, and Israel experiences for young people and cites the value of "social justice, community service and other forms of activism" to "reinforce Jewish social networks among young adults."

Cohen sees outreach as "minimalist" by comparison. He notes, however, that where non-Jews engage in Jewish life (with or without conversion), rates of Jewish involvement approach those of inmarriage. Cohen recommends "a philanthropically funded rabbinic conversion corps" to "send a message that the Jewish community encourages and welcomes conversion."

In the end, says Cohen, policy makers need to put the focus on enlarging participation in Jewish educational activities of all kinds, "focused on texts, cultural engagement, social justice activities, or spiritual experiences."

The Greater Boston Community Study: Intermarried Families and Their Children

T HIS REPORT, USING DATA FROM A 2005 STUDY OF THE GREATER BOSTON JEWISH community, found that 60 percent of the children born to intermarried families are being raised "solely Jewish."[1] This figure is markedly higher than percentages recorded in other American Jewish communities. The 2000–01 National Jewish Population Survey, for example, reports 33 to 39 percent nationally.[2] The Boston study also shows that intermarried families choosing to raise their children as Jews "are generally as observant as inmarried Jewish families, especially Reform families, and their children become B'nai Mitzvah at the same rates."

In his foreword to the March 2008 report, Barry Shrage, president of Combined Jewish Philanthropies, explained the community's successful approach:

> As Jews in America in the twenty-first century, we live in a world of almost infinite choice. One of these choices now includes religious identity and affiliation. As some have termed it, we are all "Jews by choice." Many of us live far away from the communities in which we were raised and we often intermarry. It seems likely that, in the near future, over half of the children born in Jewish households will be born to intermarried parents. We also live in a world of contradiction; even as identity has become more fluid, people are increasingly searching for a community of values and meaning.
>
> Ten years ago, in our last strategic plan, Combined Jewish Philanthropies made two decisions that reflected our awareness of these trends. First, we decided to make the Greater Boston Jewish community much more welcoming to interfaith families . . .[and] dramatically increased our support of programming for interfaith families. Being inclusive became one of our key strategic priorities.

In parallel, we also embarked on a series of initiatives designed to increase the overall vibrancy of the Jewish community. We invested in adult Jewish learning and literacy, in family educators in synagogues, in our day schools, and in a wide variety of other programs. In this way, our efforts in Boston to welcome intermarried families have been part of a larger vision to support a Jewish community that is appealing, meaningful and accessible. . . .

In a time of choice, participation for all Jews, whether single, inmarried or intermarried, depends on how compelling and accessible the opportunities are. By combining a universal desire for values with warmth and openness, we can create a world of meaning and beauty that will make Jewish choices compelling for all of our children and grandchildren.

Chapter Notes

1. *The 2005 Greater Boston Community Study: Intermarried Families and Their Children.* A Report of Combined Jewish Philanthropies. March 2008. www.cjp.org/communitystudy

2. "The National Jewish Population Survey 2000–01: Strength, Challenge and Diversity in the American Jewish Population." A United Jewish Communities Report in Cooperation with the Mandell L. Berman Institute – North American Jewish Data Bank, September 2003, updated January 2004. http://www.jewishfederations.org/local_includes/downloads/4606.pdf

CHAPTER EIGHT

The Voices of Women

Barbara Z. Koppel

Temple Emanu-El, WRJ

With comments by Rabbi Marla Feldman

Executive Director, Women of Reform Judaism

"The emergence of women as full partners in the enhancement of Judaism has been one of the most profound changes that have transformed Jewish life in our times."

— *1987 Annual Report of the UAHC*

T HE YEAR WAS 1987. ON A FRIDAY NIGHT DURING PASSOVER, A CONTINGENT of women who called themselves *Kol Nashim* (Voice of Women) conducted Temple Emanu-El's first egalitarian *erev Shabbat* service. Only women, many wearing *kipot* and *tallitot*, ascended the *bimah* that night. They read Torah, spoke about women in Judaism, and led the congregation in prayer and song. In the service itself, translations of the Hebrew prayers portrayed God as a Transcendent Being without gender.[1]

The experience of compiling the Shabbat service was so powerful for the group that *Kol Nashim* continued as a women's study group, creating a women's seder and, ultimately, under the leadership of Temple Emanu-El's Vivian Newmark, a special *haggadah*.

The *Kol Nashim* service was a defining moment for Temple Emanu-El, yet it was also a natural progression in the evolution of women's leadership at the synagogue.

Ever since 1950, when Ruth Millman convened a group of Westfield women to discuss the founding of a temple, women have played a pivotal role in the life of Temple Emanu-El.

In earlier years, the Sisterhood provided a way for women to engage in synagogue life, support Jewish religious and educational values, and come together as a community. Today, women have the option to engage in congregational life professionally, through Sisterhood, or as part of the broader Temple leadership.

Women of Reform Judaism: "Meeting women where they are."

THE REFORM MOVEMENT'S WOMEN OF REFORM JUDAISM (WRJ) REMAINS A vital force in liberal Jewish life throughout the world. Founded in 1913 as the National Federation of Temple Sisterhoods (NFTS), WRJ has a distinguished history of activism, education, and financial support that continues to this day. As Jan Epstein, former URJ regional president and Honorary Life Member, URJ board of governors, reports, the preamble to the 1913 NFTS constitution recognized this important role from the very beginning: "The increased power which has come to the modern American Jewess ought to be exercised in congregational life."[2]

The women of NFTS marched for women's rights, cared for immigrants after World War I, supported rabbinical students, spoke out on issues of health, education, and social justice, raised money through the Youth, Education, and Special Projects (YES) Fund, helped found the Jewish Braille Institute, provided the funding for Reform Judaism's first home in New York, were instrumental in the founding of the North American Federation of Temple Youth (NFTY), and helped promote liberal Judaism worldwide.

In 1933 Jane Evans was named the first full-time director of NFTS. Known as "the first lady of Reform Judaism," Evans was "[the] moving force in charting new directions for NFTS. . . . In 1951, just as President John F. Kennedy was convening the Commission on the Status of Women, Evans brought the question of women's rabbinic ordination before NFTS. Under her guidance, resolutions supporting access to birth control information, civil rights, fair employment practices, child labor legislation, the revision of immigration legislation, the elimination of capital punishment, and the de-escalation of the Vietnam War were all endorsed at NFTS biennial conventions."[3]

Evans and her successors, Eleanor Schwartz (1976–1992), Ellen Y. Rosenberg (1992–2003), and Shelley Lindauer (2004–11), took WRJ "far beyond the domestic sphere of its founders into the larger Jewish world and arena of women and politics."[4] One of the organization's most far-reaching projects is *The Torah: A Women's Commentary*,[5] published in 2008 by the URJ Press with WRJ support. As Rosanne Selfon, then WRJ president, notes in her foreword to the *Commentary*, Cantor Sarah Sager, a leader in the effort to create this work, "planted a seed, claiming that women could create a Torah commentary that would incorporate women's experiences and women's history into the living memory of our people."[6] That volume, featuring Torah commentaries written by more than 150 Jewish women — rabbis, cantors, educators, scholars, and archaeologists — is now a staple of Torah study worldwide.

Today, Selfon reports, under the leadership of Rabbi Marla Feldman, WRJ continues to broaden its support for the next generation of Jewish involvement, funding scholarships for Reform Jewish camps, legislative assistants at the Religious Action Center in Washington, the URJ Campaign for Youth Engagement, and Reform rabbinic students throughout the world.[7]

At Emanu-El, the Sisterhood continues to play an important role in the Temple's life, helping with holiday celebrations, supporting the Religious School, and serving as a training ground for congregational leadership. At the same time, it reflects the significant changes that have occurred since women were first permitted to participate to a degree not previously seen.

Arlene Burstein, long active in Sisterhood, remembers what it meant to women of her generation: "I attended my first Sisterhood board meeting because I could go out to lunch with the ladies and have free reliable babysitting. Women were home with children and looking for meaningful and stimulating ways to spend time. Now, with so many choices and obligations and limited free time, I see many capable young women opting straight for the Temple board."

Societal changes have come so swiftly and with so much challenge that women are bombarded with choices. They can choose to be at home, in a career, or both. Similarly, the relationship between men and women is changing as they seek ways to participate in Temple life as a family.

Miriam Silver Verga says she and her husband sought out the opposite of a Sisterhood/Men's Club division. "Those of us who are intermarried need a social situation that is egalitarian." She looks for ways women and men can work together. LINKS, the group that evolved from the Early Childhood Education program, has been instrumental in unifying men and women into what Miriam refers to as an "open" *chavurah*. "It's not about women; it's about incorporating both sides equally."

URJ President Emeritus Rabbi Eric Yoffie spoke to WRJ in 2011. Many people had advised him that, with temple leadership open to women, Sisterhoods were no longer needed. "My gut told me they were wrong," he said and gave his reasons. "They underestimate the quality of your leadership . . . [and] your capacity to reinvent yourselves as an organization." They also miss that "Jewish women are still going to want to come together as women, and to do certain things as women." Finally, he noted, they misread "the unique role that Sisterhood had played, and continues to play, in the history of Reform Judaism."[8]

Rabbi Feldman echoes that thought. "We've found that young women have the same hunger to bond with other women as their older counterparts. We want to create a safe space for women of all ages and interests to get together, while respecting the uniqueness of each community."

The *Lilith* Salon, a partnership between the Jewish feminist magazine and WRJ, is one example. Another, "Girls' Night Out," provides opportunities for good times and camaraderie while raising funds for temple programs. "The most successful programs are not 'top down' but meet women where they are," says Rabbi Feldman.

WRJ has proved especially important for interfaith families. Whether raised in another faith or born Jewish but lacking a background in Judaism, women can come together to teach and learn about the tradition. One of the most valuable ways to transmit Jewish values and traditions has been through cookbooks, a signature program for Temple Emanu-El and for Sisterhoods through the ages, replete with family recipes, photos, and personal memories.

"We are, indeed, 'Stronger Together,'" says Rabbi Feldman, as WRJ marks its 2013 Centennial.

The Changing Face of Temple Leadership: "Keep your father's commandments, and do not forsake your mother's Torah." Proverbs 6:20

T HE SOCIETAL CHANGES OF THE 1970S HAD A POWERFUL IMPACT. IN 1969, NFTS called upon the URJ (then UAHC) to set up a task force on Reform Jewish women as a way to open membership on the Union board and promote women for president, vice president, and treasurer of their congregations. Until then, the only temple board position most women held was that of secretary. The task force was established in 1970.[9]

A decade later, the same year Ellen Lewis became the first Emanu-El woman ordained as a rabbi, Zelda Kahn became the first woman president at the Temple and also the first in New Jersey. Zelda joined the Temple board in 1967 as Sisterhood president, continuing her board presence in various capacities for 17 years.

Zelda truly broke the mold. Active on regional, national, and even global levels, Zelda set new precedents both within Emanu-El and in the Reform world at large. An NFTS board member from 1976-1980, Zelda also served as NFTS New Jersey Federation president; vice president of the New Jersey Region of the Union; temple board trainer for the state; fund-raising chair for the World Union for Progressive Judaism (WUPJ); vice president for membership, Association of Reform Zionists of America (ARZA); and delegate to the World Zionist Congress in 1986. Active beyond the Jewish world, she also co-chaired the New York–New Jersey Coalition for Abortion Rights.

At the same time that women rose to leadership positions within the synagogue, they continued to fill traditional roles. Zelda recalls, "Women brought their blenders to the Temple kitchen to prepare potato pancakes for Religious School children. They decorated the *sukkah* and the *bimah* for holidays. The Friendship Group was made up of senior citizens (mostly women) who met once a month for a lunch provided by women who came and cooked for and served the group."

Eileen Nathanson, the first Sisterhood president to sit on the executive board, took over the reins of the Temple presidency in 1982. "Women did not hold the Torah in the early times," she notes. "We sat on the *bimah*, but that was all."

Elaine Weill became the next woman president in 1990. Her personal journey, from an upbringing in an Orthodox *shul* to the leadership of a Reform synagogue, reveals how quickly nontraditional opportunities became available for women once the momentum began. "As women began moving into leadership positions at Temple Emanu-El, I was invited to join the board of trustees," Elaine comments. "The interaction of board members . . . was women and men on equal footing, both devoted to the common goal of moving our synagogue forward in a positive way. . . . I frequently wondered how, in the past, this had been possible without the contribution of a female perspective."

Elaine was followed by Phyllis Buchsbaum in 1996, who was motivated by her adult bat mitzvah experience. Looking to the future, Phyllis says, "I see more mixing of faiths and races. If we want to keep the Jewish community vital, I feel strongly that we have to embrace this blending and make the Temple feel like home to these families."

Terri Klass, Marci Schoenbach, and Gail Friedman followed. When Marci joined the congregation in 1989, the first place she encountered women at Emanu-El was in the nursery school. She found "women active and in power" and notes "that has continued."

Women in Religious Leadership: "God continues to speak to each generation; in this one, we hear women's voices."
Ellen Umansky, "Women and Contemporary Revelation,"
The Torah: A Women's Commentary

IN THE 1920s, THE DAUGHTER OF AN HUC PROFESSOR WANTED TO BECOME A Reform rabbi. Two rabbis on the eight-man board of governors voted in favor but were defeated. In the early 1950s, NFTS adopted a resolution about women in the rabbinate following informal negotiations with HUC president Dr. Nelson Glueck, who favored it. According to Jan Epstein, several qualified women studied at HUC, "but the faculty did not vote to ordain them, hoping and praying they would fall in love with and marry male rabbinic students and therefore beg the question."[10]

The Reform Movement ultimately laid a solid foundation for gender equality with the ordination in 1972 of Sally Preisand, the first woman rabbi, and with the investiture in 1975 of Barbara Ostfeld-Horowitz, the first female cantor. In the decade from 2002 to 2011, 256 women, 57 percent of all graduating classes, were ordained.[11]

At Emanu-El, Annette Rindner achieved another kind of milestone. In 1970 she became the first woman called for an *aliyah*. Around that time women, along with men, were trained to conduct *minyanim* in the homes of families observing *shiva*. While this was not universally accepted in the beginning, even when women rabbis conducted the service, it eventually became the norm.

Most women in these early years had childhood memories of brothers becoming bar mitzvah with no parallel ceremony for them. In 1974, another landmark year, an adult bat mitzvah class formed to fill that gap. After two years of intensive Jewish study, 22 women celebrated the first adult bat mitzvah ceremony at Temple Emanu-El.

Rabbi Susan Friedman, a former congregant who was ordained in 1996, offers her insights into the changing religious roles of women: "I joined Temple Emanu-El in 1983. By that time, it seemed to me that many roads to leadership were available to women. The only deterrent seemed to be the prayer language, which was clearly masculine. In 1986, it did not feel like a casual decision whether to wear a *tallit* or a *kipah*. To do so felt, for me, like a revolutionary act." Rabbi Friedman recalls a Shabbat morning *minyan* when she suddenly found herself carrying the Torah around and managing its physicality. "I realized that in my entire life, and by then I was near 50, I had never done that and was filled with awe."

In 1986, Martha Novick became the first woman cantor at Emanu-El. The first woman rabbi, Deborah Joselow, came on board in 1991, serving as assistant rabbi until 1996. Her comments on the role of women provide insight into the ongoing changes in Temple life:

> By the time I arrived in 1991, there were so many wonderful women in leadership positions. For me in particular, Zelda Kahn, Eileen Nathanson, and Elaine Weill stood out. So the "first" business seemed superficial. Except of course it wasn't. What I discovered is that in lots of big and important ways, the Temple was a model for promoting women. All kinds of fundamental ceilings had been smashed. Cantor Novick had been on the pulpit way before I showed up.
>
> The real revolution was in the little things, and the real surprise was in the synagogue's struggle to turn the small corners. The lesson I learned

was in the importance of attending to the basics — like parenting leave and equal pay. No one wants to be "other," even if that otherness is a moment of tremendous excitement and enthusiasm, which is certainly how I was, for the most part, greeted.

A number of women served as assistant rabbis at Emanu-El. By the time Erin Glazer became assistant rabbi in 2009, the role of women had changed considerably. Together with Cantor Novick, Rabbi Glazer, now associate rabbi, and Rabbi Sarah Smiley, who came to Emanu-El in 2011, women now constitute three-quarters of the *bimah* presence with Rabbi Sagal.

There were many milestones for women associated with Temple Emanu-El. In addition to Ellen Lewis and Susan Friedman, others ordained as rabbis include Jacquie Tattenbaum Satlow, Jill Maderer, Elisa Koppel, Mara Judd Young, and Rachel Ackerman. Jennifer Kanarek Cahn was invested as a cantor. Helga Newmark, director of the Temple's Religious School from 1982 to 1989, was then the oldest woman and the last Holocaust survivor to be ordained as a rabbi by HUC-JIR.

Jill Spasser, who led the Emanu-El choir for more than 10 years as a volunteer and started the youth choir, became a cantor and served on the faculty of the HUC-JIR School of Sacred Music. Countless other women connected to Temple Emanu-El are leaders, both paid and volunteer, in Jewish communities throughout the world.

Rabbi Elisa Koppel, who grew up at Temple Emanu-El and was ordained in 2001, observes that changes regarding women were more subtle than surprising:

Zelda Kahn becoming the first female president of the Temple seemed something that of course a female could do. I never really understood the need for Kol Nashim or other such projects because in my world view, women could do anything men could. The hiring of Martha Novick as cantor was probably the biggest change that I noticed. Looking back, a female being hired as senior clergy in a large and influential congregation was a huge step. I didn't realize the significance at the time. It's nice to know that my home congregation was forward-thinking in this regard.

I'd like to see things even out so that the role of women as I perceived it to be in my younger years is, in fact, how it is.

As Rabbi Joselow expresses it: "We will all have arrived in the Promised Land when whoever we are — by gender, race, intellectual, or physical ability — is inconsequential to the fact that we were made in the image of God and are eager to offer our best selves in service to our community."

In this chapter, we honor women members of Temple Emanu-El and the many more unsung women of our Temple who moved forward to establish their own interpretation of Torah values through their commitment to Judaism. Much like the interpretations of the scholars in the *Commentary*, our women clergy, Sisterhood members, synagogue leadership, and women at large have changed the Temple Emanu-El model and helped to create a welcoming, gender-neutral synagogue community. In her preface to the *Commentary*, Cantor Sager mentions her discovery that the scholarly work of Torah commentary was ". . . opening the door to restoring a sense of women's presence at the most important moments of our history and in our most sacred text."[12] The women of this chapter and the many who are unnamed had broken this ground years earlier.

May it therefore continue to be that our Temple Emanu-El community, women and men alike, will follow in the footsteps of those women who have come before us. May we continue to seek a broader and even more inclusive interpretation of the life of the individual and the community as reflected in our Torah values.

Kein Ye'hi Ratzon

Chapter Notes

1. Terry Kroloff, PhD, "The Road to Gender Equality at Temple Emanu-El and Beyond," 2003. This report is a key source for much of the early history of women's participation at Temple Emanu-El included in this chapter.

2. Jan Epstein, sermon on the role of women in Jewish history and American Reform Judaism, delivered at an NFTS national convention in Atlanta during her presidency of the URJ Southeast Region. The first woman to serve as president of an Atlanta synagogue (1978–80), Epstein has been a member of the URJ board since 1981 and is active in a number of joint CCAR-URJ commissions and local organizations.

3. Pamela S. Nadell, "National Federation of Temple Sisterhoods," *Jewish Women: A Comprehensive Historical Encyclopedia*, 20 March 2009. Jewish Women's Archive. http://jwa.org/encyclopedia/article/national-federation-of-temple-sisterhoods

4. Ibid.

5. Tamara Cohn Eskenazi, editor; Andrea L. Weiss, associate editor. *The Torah: A Women's Commentary* (New York: URJ Press and Women of Reform Judaism, 2008).

6. Ibid., xxv.

7. Rosanne M. Selfon, WRJ Immediate Past President, "Women of Reform Judaism: 100-Year Legacy," sermon delivered on February 24, 2012, 5.

8. Selfon, 7.

9. Epstein, 13.

10. Ibid., 10-11.

11. HUC-JIR Database 2012.

12. *Women's Commentary*, xxvii.

Through the Decades

A visual history of Temple Emanu-El's commitment to learning, praying, and doing justly.

1951: Groundbreaking for Temple Emanu-El's first building. Left to right: Rabbi Ezra Spicehandler, Jack Klion, Josh Shapiro, Ruth Millman, Sol Silberman, Bernard Bernstein.

Through the Decades

Reception

Tendered by the Sisterhood, Temple Emanu-El

MR. N. STRITZLER ....Toast Master

RABBI EZRA SPICEHANDLER ....Opening Benediction

REMARKS ....Mr. Stritzler, Chairman

MR. JULIAN LEVY ....Chairman Building Com.

RABBI EZRA SPICEHANDLER ....Temple Emanu-El

MRS. KARL MILLMANN ....President, Sisterhood,
Temple Emanu-El

MR. DAVID SCHIMMEL ......President, Temple Emanu-El

RABBI MARTIN FRIEDMAN, Elizabeth......Closing Benediction

Reception: American Legion Hall, 1003 W. North Av., Westfield

Temple Emanu-El, Westfield

DECEMBER 9, 1951

Ground-Breaking Ceremony

"AMERICA" ....Cantor Marshall Glatzer
Temple Emanu-El

BENEDICTION ....Rabbi Jordon Taxon
Temple Beth-El, Cranford

REMARKS ....Mr. David Schimmel
President, Temple Emanu-El

GREETINGS ....Mayor Charles Bailey
Westfield, New Jersey

The Rev. Frederick Blatz
Pres. Westfield Ministerium

The Rev. Dr. J. L. McCorison
First Congregational Church, Westfield

ADDRESS ....Rabbi Sidney Nathanson
Temple B'nai Sholom, Plainfield

MESSAGE ....Mrs. Karl Millmann
President, Sisterhood, Temple Emanu-El

Ground-Breaking Service

RABBI EZRA SPICEHANDLER......Temple Emanu-El, Westfield

THE BREAKING OF GROUND ....Mr. Julian Levy
Chairman Building Committee

Mrs. Millmann

Mr. Schimmel

CLOSING BENEDICTION ....Rabbi Theodore B. Haberstadter
Elmora Hebrew Center, Elizabeth

1951: Program for Groundbreaking.

1953: The first Temple Emanu-El.

Through the Decades

1967: Bea Reiss, Annette Rindner, and Betty Barnett plan the first Sisterhood Craft Show, an annual event for many years.

1970: Rabbi Kroloff leads Soviet Jewry rally on East Broad Street, Westfield. (Photo: Jack Rindner)

1970: Jeanne Goldstein and Irene Buchner (right rear) march through downtown Westfield in support of Soviet Jewry.

Through the Decades

1974: Beloved Emanu-El Nursery School teacher Lisbeth Brodie
gives a special hug to one of her students.

1978: Temple Emanu-El youth groupers relaxing on the lawn.

Through the Decades

▲ **1980:** Evelyn Averick presents Rabbi Kroloff with her commemorative book, *A Historic Narrative: The Story of Temple Emanu-El, Westfield, New Jersey: In Honor of the 30th Anniversary, 1950-1980.*

◄ **1986:** Father Leroy Lyons and Rabbi Kroloff proudly display *The Pajama Game* program.

Through the Decades

1986: Stars of *The Pajama Game*, a joint production staged by ARK partners Temple Emanu-El and St. Mark's Episcopal Church, Plainfield. Left to right: Bill Coleman, Jr., Lisa Logan, Lauren Shub, Gerry Cantor, Debbie Shapiro, Mel Cohen, and Bonnie Rapp. (Photo: Susan Kreitzer)

1986: Temple Emanu-El marches in Washington with the Religious Coalition for Abortion Rights (RCAR). Left to right, Myra Terry, Elisha Monzella, Bettye Barcan, Sarah Kroloff, Ruth Kreisman, Bonnie Forgash, and Jane Raeter. (Photo: Charlotte Gelfand)

Through the Decades

1988: Harris Gilbert and fellow ARK volunteers from
St. Mark's Episcopal Church rehab a house in Plainfield.

1988: ARK Board: Back row, left to right, Sally Gilbert, Ken Sumner,
Harris Gilbert, Lewis Coe, Roger Asch, Ed Danner, Dennis Williams. Front row,
left to right: Jacquie Sumner, Terry Kroloff, Father Lyons, Jacqui Rose.

Through the Decades

▲ **1990:** Alan Dershowitz (center) speaks at Temple Emanu-El Adult Education program. Welcoming him, left to right: Rabbi Kroloff, Alan Goldstein, Bob Tell, Dershowitz, Walter Averick, Elaine Weill, Evelyn Averick, Beverly Warmbrand, and the Honorable Al Wolin.

▶ **Mid-1990's:** Mitzvah Day Cleanup Project.

Through the Decades

▲ **2000:** Groundbreaking for the Rabbi Charles A. Kroloff Center for Jewish Learning. Left to right: Emanu-El student Josh Schwartz, Steve Rosenberg, Mitzi Eisenberg, Adam Bengal, Warren Eisenberg, Cantor Novick, Rabbi Kroloff, Dr. Stan Gersch, and Bill Maderer.

◀ **2002:** Sarah Liebowitz and William Schoenbach, volunteers with the first Mandy Reichman Feeding Program turkey drive, help deliver food to the needy.

Through the Decades

2002: Emanu-El graduates and friends honor Rabbi Kroloff at a special Retirement Shabbat. Left to right: Rabbi Ellen Lewis, Rabbi Robert Samuels, Rabbi Kroloff, Rabbi (and former Education Director) Helga Newmark, Rabbi David Wechsler-Azen, Rabbi Jill Maderer, and Rabbi Elisa Koppel.

2003: David Schulman, Men's Club Sukkah-building team.

Early 2000's: Gerry Cantor helps Religious School student shake the *lulav* for *Sukkot*.

Through the Decades

2004: Sisterhood and other Pro-Choice Marchers, Washington, DC: Laurie Goldsmith Heitner, Jackie Bass, Charlotte Gelfand, Suzi Shane, Nanci Pompan, Carolyn Shane, and Alyssa Shane.

2004: Emanu-El Religious School student packs lunches for the needy as part of the Mandy Reichman Feeding Program.

2000's: Cantor Martha Novick leads the congregation in spirited singing.

Through the Decades

2005: Hannah Lieberman (left), Marlene Maderer (center), and Meryl Reichman (right) knit Blankets of Love for children with cancer.

2008: Rabbi Sagal and Michael Glickstein share a moment during a Purim celebration. Michael participated in the Temple Emanu-El and Jewish Federation of Greater MetroWest Ma'ayan program, providing Jewish education and enrichment for children with special needs.

Through the Decades

2008: Rabbi Sagal and Judith Langholtz get into the Shabbat Hallelu spirit.

2010: 50th anniversary of Rabbi Kroloff's ordination. Left to right, front row: Rabbis Jill Maderer, Elisa Koppel, Eric Yoffie, Charles A. Kroloff, Doug Sagal, and Lenny Thal. Second row: Peri Smilow, Rabbis Erin Glazer, Arnie Gluck, Ellen Lewis, Marc Disick, and Rex Perlmeter.

Through the Decades

2
0
1
0
'S

LEARN
PRAY
DO JUSTLY

2011: Rabbi Marcus Burstein (left) and Bernie Weinstein by the campfire at the annual Men's Club Retreat.

▲ **2012:** "I Have a Dream" graduates with college destination T-shirts.

2003: Members of "I Have a Dream" entering class, with Rabbi Kroloff. (Photos: courtesy Larry Leverett)

Through the Decades

2012: Religious School student Zachary Marcus and Rabbi Erin Glazer tend to the Mitzvah Garden lettuce crop.

2013: The Tuesday Morning Bible Class celebrates Rabbi Sagal's 10th anniversary of leadership.

2013: Cantor Novick (front row, center) and students in Emanu-El's Gesher L'Kesher program at Celebration Oaks Park in New Orleans, where they volunteered for park cleanup and other projects in the hurricane-devastated Lower Ninth Ward.

Through the Decades

Amy Levitt celebrates receiving her first Torah.

Emanu-El's distinctive Torah covers, created by New Jersey fiber artist and Temple member Ina Golub, whose custom-designed Judaica is found throughout the U.S. and in Israel.

CHAPTER NINE

Hinei Ma Tov: The Warmth and Power of Men's Fellowship

The Role of Men in Jewish Life: A Conversation with Rabbi Jeffrey K. Salkin

T HE ROLE OF MEN IN JEWISH LIFE WAS RARELY IN QUESTION THROUGHOUT MOST of Jewish history. Men and women understood their roles and what was expected of them. In today's liberal Judaism, however, traditional norms have shifted. Women have become central to the institutions of American Jewish life. They are ordained as rabbis and cantors, lead synagogues, teach, and write Torah commentaries. Studies show the shift to strong participation by women is accompanied by a declining involvement of men.[1] This is particularly true for the crucial teen years. Young women predominate in post–b'nei mitzvah classes, youth groups, camping, and other programs aimed at Jewish teens.

So it is interesting to take a closer look at the broader issues confronting liberal Jewish institutions when it comes to attracting men. Rabbi Jeffrey K. Salkin, a leading commentator on Jewish life, author of *Searching for My Brothers: Jewish Men in a*

Gentile World[2] and editor of *The Modern Men's Torah Commentary*,[3] sees the challenges as an opportunity. One of the values of the feminist movement, he says, is that it sensitizes us to look more deeply into what it means to be a Jewish man and to define Judaism's particular "style" of masculinity. His anthology of Torah commentaries by rabbis and other men active in Jewish life speaks to what men can learn from Jewish sources about such issues as family, work-life balance, spirituality, ethics, aggression, health, body image, sexuality, aging, and death.

Rabbi Salkin traces the three eras of how masculinity has been defined in Jewish history. In the Bible, men held positions of power as kings, priests, and prophets. But that power never went unchecked. Biblical law placed limits on masculine privilege in such areas as the use of power, even the king's, and the treatment of slaves and women.

After 70 CE, in the wake of the destruction of the Temple and the loss of their land, sovereignty, and national independence, Jews were faced with a dilemma. Unable to "fight back," the quintessential role of men, they redefined masculinity and male responsibility. For centuries thereafter, rabbinic leaders elevated other aspects of the masculine personality, particularly study, community, and compassion, making those the defining factors, says Rabbi Salkin. The challenge became, "How much Talmud can you learn?"

Since 1948, when the modern State of Israel was proclaimed, the equation changed once again. Zionism brought about the "remasculinization" of Jewish men. The Maccabees became the paragon of manhood (historical reality notwithstanding), and what was perceived as the feminized, weakened men of the Diaspora was rejected. Even Golda Meir was praised for her "manly" qualities. Rabbi Salkin observes that this view of manhood, which now seems dated, persists in many corners of the Jewish world and consciousness.

Today, as liberal Jews search for a creative synthesis of masculine and feminine sensibilities, the scales have tipped in the other direction. At the same time as women have risen to positions of power, men have "wandered away," according to Rabbi Salkin. Many synagogue services are shaped by a more feminine sensibility, he says, and skills thought to be necessary for synagogue leadership are perceived to be "items in an emotional toolbox that men stereotypically don't have."

Rabbi Salkin's concerns are shared by the Reform Movement. The North American Federation of Temple Brotherhoods (NFTB), founded in 1923, officially changed its name in 2007 to Men of Reform Judaism (MRJ). The organization's mission has broadened to include "men's fellowship, interest in Jewish worship, Jewish studies, *tikkun olam* and service to the congregation, Jewish community and the community at large."[4] MRJ encompasses everything from traditional Temple Brotherhoods and Men's Clubs to *chavurot*, study groups, and online communities. MRJ program modules, like the *BenAbbaZeyde* (son/father/grandfather) project and the Men's Seder, are designed to give men "space" to rediscover how Judaism can speak to them as well as opportunities to experience "warmth and the power of fellowship."

Temple Emanu-El Men's Club: Reshaping the Mission

Mike Hamerman

Temple Emanu-El Men's Club

THE MEN'S CLUB STILL SERVES ITS TRADITIONAL ROLE AS ONE OF EMANU-EL'S major fund-raising arms. We organize community blood drives and food delivery to the needy, support the purchase and repair of Torahs, meet the Temple's building-related needs, and update the Temple Emanu-El Journal each year. We build the Temple *sukkah*, host the Chanukah dinner, put on the Purim Carnival, and, together with LINKS, our young families group, organize the annual Temple picnic.

Emanu-El has grappled with many of the challenges to which Rabbi Salkin refers in varying degrees. For me, however, the Men's Club has been successful in giving us a chance to bond with our peers and create friendships that last for many years. Like Sisterhood, Men's Club was a close-knit family 30-plus years ago when I became a member, and to a great degree it remains that way. In my experience, the men of Men's Club and the women of Sisterhood have always worked closely together and on equal footing to support the Temple and the wider community.

My own engagement goes back to 1978, when my wife and I became Temple members. I joined Men's Club under the extraordinary leadership of Jerry Linder and have remained a very active member, holding almost every Men's Club office, including that of president (2004–06). In addition to Jerry, I have been privileged to work with such notable leaders as Mel Cohen, Herb Ross, Lou Tischler, Bob Mansfeld, and our current president, Marc Epstein.

Although members of Men's Club are giving, caring men willing and ready to aid the Temple in so many ways, national trends have clearly affected us. When I was a fledgling member, 35 to 40 men attended our monthly meetings. Today the numbers have declined. Younger members are willing to work on specific projects, but many find that a long-term commitment to Men's Club is just not possible.

Commenting on these trends, Rabbi Salkin observes that many synagogues need to reshape and re-imagine how synagogues serve their members, fostering affinity groups that grow organically from people's needs. At Temple Emanu-El, we are already on that track with such programs as LINKS. At the same time, there is no question that men still need opportunities to connect with each other just as women do.

As Rabbi Salkin also notes, "Many men are still looking for places to hang out with men, a place where they can have masculine friendships without looking like a 'no-girls-allowed clubhouse.'" That is the genesis of our Men's Club Retreat.

Men's Club Retreat: Torah, Song, Laughter, Talk . . . and Poker

IN 2004, AS I WAS PREPARING FOR MY MEN'S CLUB PRESIDENCY, I WANTED TO COME up with a special activity that would help the men bond. How could we achieve this? Rabbi Sagal had the answer — a retreat, complete with rabbi and song leader. I gladly took this on with the help of fellow Men's Club members David Gelber, Len Traiman, and Pete Klein.

It worked better than we ever imagined. In 2013 we marked the tenth anniversary of the retreat, held each year just before the High Holy Days at Camp Louemma in Sussex, New Jersey. A truly intergenerational group, about 18 to 25 men ranging in age from early 40s to mid-80s attend each year.

From Friday afternoon through Saturday night, ending with *Havdalah*, the men enjoy the incomparable experience of a kosher camp Shabbat as adults, including Shabbat dinner, services, discussions, singing, praying, relaxing, outdoor activities, and, of course, a campfire with marshmallows and s'mores. Temple Emanu-El's own Barry Merer is our song leader *extraordinaire*, as we engage in spirited prayer and singing. Everyone participates in the Shabbat morning Torah service. Four Torah readers chant, thanks to CDs Cantor Novick has graciously prepared in advance. For some of the men, this may be a new experience. Imagine the first-time thrill of removing the Torah from the ark and walking with it as fellow worshippers touch it lovingly with their *tzitzit*.

The retreat enables the men to experience the beauty of a peaceful Shabbat shared with friends in a magnificent setting. I know from the depth and breadth of the discussions that the men appreciate this rare opportunity for introspection and insight while bonding with each other. The retreat offers men what Rabbi Salkin sees as the need to talk about their lives, their hopes, and their dreams in a context where other men won't judge. "There are so few places outside the therapist's office where men can talk about topics like careers, families, relationships, and aging," he says.

Our discussion leaders have brought this openness to our gatherings. Rabbi John Fishman provided expert leadership and stability for our fledgling program. Rabbi Josh Cantor, a longtime congregant and beloved *minyan* leader, ably followed for a year. Our discussion leader for the past several years was Rabbi Marcus Burstein, who brought a warm, gentle leadership to the event.[5] Recently, the leadership role was filled by Razi Haime-Cohen, an engaging, knowledgeable Emanu-El congregant and seasoned Jewish workshop leader.

The experience has great value not just for us but also for our discussion leaders. Rabbi Burstein says, "I have known some of the men who attended for my entire life. It was special for me to have a completely different role from when I was a boy. My teachers and other adults I had looked up to growing up now looked to me as their teacher, which was a humbling experience."

He sees the appeal of the retreat as a combination of adult intellectual and spiritual activity and a rare opportunity for male friendship: "It was an unusual combination of men interested in Jewish prayer and learning who also stay up for hours past midnight playing poker, joking, and having a good time."

Stan Biner, a former Men's Club president, underscores this winning combination. "I look forward to [the retreats], to the camaraderie and the chance to hang out with people one doesn't get a chance to hang out with during the year. We have fun, and talk, and pray, and read Torah. And we learn something new each year."[6]

It is meaningful to me that the men share their thoughts and feelings so openly, especially since we meet right before the High Holy Days. The sharing enhances our social and spiritual bonding. It's that feeling of holiness that means so much to me and keeps me engaged.

It may seem new, but in fact, the retreat and Men's Club itself help us renew and reshape an age-old rabbinic tradition. As Rabbi Salkin describes it, "For generations, Jewish men found their 'macho' in mastery of Torah, in heartfelt worship, and in feats of lovingkindness and charity. True Jewish masculine power was, and is, not a fist but an open heart and open hand."[7]

Chapter Notes

1. Sylvia Barack Fishman and Daniel Parmer, "Matrilineal Ascent/Patrilineal Descent: The Growing Gender Imbalance in American Jewish Life." Maurice and Marilyn Cohen Center for Modern Jewish Studies. Boston: Brandeis University, 2008. Cited in Rabbi Jeffrey K. Salkin, *The Modern Men's Torah Commentary: New Insights from Jewish Men on the 54 Weekly Torah Portions* (Woodstock, Vt.: Jewish Lights Publishing, 2009), xvi.

2. Penguin Putnam (1999).

3. Salkin, *Modern Men's Torah Commentary*, xvi.

4. www.mrj.org.

5. Our discussion leaders all have strong ties to Emanu-El. Rabbi Fishman is the husband of our former assistant rabbi, Jennifer Clayman. Rabbi Cantor's parents, Gerry and Dorothy, are Emanu-El stalwarts, and Rabbi Burstein's parents, Arlene and Julie, served as Sisterhood and Men's Club presidents.

6. Elaine Durbach, "Men share Shabbat away from home: Emanu-El retreat aims to inspire spirituality and fellowship," New Jersey Jewish News, Sept. 21, 2011. http://www.njjewishnews.com/article/6560/men-shareshabbat-away-from-home#.

7. Salkin, *Modern Men's Torah Commentary*, xviii.

CHAPTER TEN

Israel, Temple Emanu-El, and the Reform Movement Strengthen the Bonds

Terry Kroloff, PhD

Temple Emanu-El

The relationship between American Reform Jews and Israel is both rewarding and challenging. This chapter looks back to an earlier time when support for the embattled state was an issue of life and death and traces the often complex relationship between American Reform Judaism and Israel through the intervening years. Temple Emanu-El's lay and rabbinic leadership, past and present, continue to play key roles in Israeli life in these difficult times.

When Everything Was on the Line

NO ONE WHO EXPERIENCED IT CAN EVER FORGET THE HEART-STOPPING DAYS OF June 5 to 10, 1967, the Six-Day War, when American Jews held their collective breath and Israel fought ferociously for her life on three fronts, battling the combined armies of Syria, Jordan, and Egypt. A week before that war began, Arab forces massed on every border of Israel and, in an act of war, closed the Straits of Tiran, blocking Israel's access to the Red Sea and beyond. At that pivotal time, more than a thousand Temple Emanu-El congregants and members of the community packed the expanded sanctuary to hear the dramatic appeal of Abba Eban, Israel's chief United

Nations representative, as it was piped in to Jews assembled throughout the country.

Congregants rose from their seats to pledge beyond their means at Israel's time of crucial need. One woman declared, "I do not have much money, but I have emptied my savings account and here it is — for Israel." This war, a turning point for Israel, which gained the Golan Heights, the West Bank, all of Jerusalem, and the Sinai Peninsula, was also transformative for Temple Emanu-El. From that event to the present, the Temple has never wavered in its commitment to the State of Israel. This commitment was underscored on Yom Kippur, 1973, when in a packed and shocked sanctuary we learned of Israel's second life-and-death struggle as Egypt and Syria launched a surprise attack across the Suez Canal and on the Golan Heights on our holiest day.

Temple Emanu-El has built its commitment to Israel not only in times of active war but also in more peaceful years. The Temple has sponsored numerous trips to Israel and programs of all types for youth and adults. The first congregational trip in 1970 delivered such an emotional charge that those travel companions continued to meet for many years after their return and even raised funds to help challenged Israeli youngsters. This visit and the many others that followed, including the 2006 three-generational, 70-person tour and a 2010 trip, have created a powerful bond to the land. According to Rabbi Sagal, Israel trips, which always include visits to Reform congregations, have also kept members informed about the growth of Israel's Reform Movement as well as the progressive activities of IRAC, the Israel Religious Action Center.

The Band's Visit

ANOTHER SIGNIFICANT ISRAEL-CENTERED EVENT OCCURRED UNEXPECTEDLY DURING the summer of 1980 when the Temple received a last-minute urgent request. When another congregation could not serve as hosts, we were asked whether we could shelter 50 Israeli youngsters and five adults for the weekend, part of a youth band visiting the United States from the village of Kiryat Ono. We answered yes, and as a result, said participating parent Jacqui Rose, "our teens had a person-to-person experience with Israeli youth" that paid dividends for years. Families hosted the young people, and five hundred individuals packed the sanctuary for the group's Sunday night concert. When the whole crew, each outfitted with a Temple Emanu-El tee shirt, drove away in their bus, both communities had gained a new appreciation of each other's lifestyle.

On June 14, 1992, we had a different kind of visit. It was standing room only when Abba Eban, Israel's former foreign minister and ambassador to the United States and the United Nations, spoke in the Greifer Sacks Hall. The county-wide Jewish community turned out 1,300-strong. Eban's eloquence and piercing intellect had a powerful impact as he explored a possible opportunity for peace in the region.

Two Communities Get Acquainted, Change the Dynamic

WHEN RABBI KROLOFF, A COMMITTED ZIONIST SINCE HIS TEENS, BECAME THE rabbi at Emanu-El in 1966, he instituted many Israel-oriented programs and strategies. Hebrew language study became required in the Religious School and an *ulpan*, or conversational Hebrew course, was offered for adults. Visits to Israel by adults and youth, often aided by substantial scholarship money, were encouraged. Young people were urged to attend the Reform Movement's summer camps with their strong Israel programming. As part of the URJ's Israel study and exchange program, several Israeli students came to live with congregant families, attending services, visiting the Religious School, joining the youth group, and becoming part of Temple Emanu-El life.

In 1987, Rabbi Kroloff, then president of the Association of Reform Zionists of America (ARZA), and Temple member Rabbi Eric Yoffie, then ARZA executive director, realized that Knesset members knew very little about the Reform Movement in the United States. They had almost no concept of the large number of Reform congregations or their influence, the nature of Reform theology, or Reform's commitment to Israel. In the Jewish State, Knesset policy has always strongly favored Orthodoxy. Orthodox congregations receive support from the state and their rabbis are salaried by the Israeli government. Orthodox Knesset members hold important seats in most ruling coalitions, Orthodox congregations are everywhere, and most Israeli families originated in lands where little was known about Reform Judaism.

With the support of Rabbi Yoffie and ARZA, Rabbi Kroloff invited contingents of Knesset members to visit Temple Emanu-El and other Reform congregations in the United States. Their agenda was to better inform Israeli Knesset members about Reform Judaism and also to help Israeli Reform rabbis struggling to perform officially recognized weddings and conversions in Israel. This program, which continued for several years, opened the eyes and minds of several Knesset members who came to the United States, attended services, and learned about the activities of Reform congregations. Temple members enjoyed the opportunity to meet and exchange ideas with members of the Knesset.

As our Emanu-El family became better acquainted with Israel, our community, led by deeply involved individual congregants, also responded to the country's financial needs. Members participate strongly in the annual UJA and Federation campaigns and generously support Israel Bonds and Hadassah medical services in Israel. Temple members have provided leadership gifts to the Brody Center for Food Sciences at the Hebrew University, Neveh Shalom Arab-Jewish village, Hand in Hand Arab-Jewish schools, NFTY-EIE High School in Israel, and many other projects to improve social services and increase understanding among Israel's diverse populations. As Emanu-El member Warren Eisenberg said, "We need to break down separation barriers wherever possible, just as we did in the United States."

A well-loved, annual part of our Yom Kippur observance continues to be the standing-room-only talk on Israeli affairs by Rabbi Eric Yoffie, URJ president emeritus. His grasp of current events and his global view of Israel's recent history make these talks a must-experience part of the High Holy Days.

One of the most indicative signs of the community's commitment to the Jewish State is the *aliyah* of several members, including Garry Bregman, Brian Gottesmann, and Chaia (Judy) Kaplan Gilbar.

Promoting Pluralism in Israel

In 1978, the Reform Movement formed ARZA in order to strengthen commitment to Israel in a grassroots and personal way for the average Reform congregant. ARZA also represents the Reform Movement's liberal, pluralistic point of view in the World Zionist Organization (WZO) in Jerusalem. In 1983, Rabbi Yoffie became the second executive director of ARZA, succeeding Rabbi Ira Youdovin, a member of Emanu-El at the time. Rabbi Yoffie generated educational material about Israel for stateside Reform rabbis and congregations, built a regional structure for ARZA, and was a strong advocate for Reform Judaism in the WZO, where he insisted that Reform and Conservative Judaism in Israel receive their fair share of WZO funding. In 1984, when Rabbi Kroloff became the president of ARZA, he continued to strengthen the organization, emphasizing the importance of a pluralistic approach to religion in Israel. During his term, a special ARZA check-off was instituted for Reform congregants' membership bills in order to ease the process of joining ARZA, a system that continues to the present.

In 1987 Rabbi Kroloff and Rabbi Yoffie decided to make a concerted effort to help Israel become a more pluralistic society. Under Israel's Law of Return, every Jew wishing to make *aliyah* was automatically granted the full rights of Israeli citizenship. However, Jews-by-choice, who had been converted to Judaism outside of Israel by non-Orthodox rabbis, were not considered Jewish in Israel. Therefore, if these new converts attempted to enter Israel under the Law of Return, they were not entitled to the full rights of citizenship, including being able to marry or be buried as Jews.

Realizing that the Religious Action Center in Washington was highly effective in promoting social action in the United States, Rabbi Kroloff, Rabbi Yoffie, and other leaders of the Reform Movement felt that a similar organization in Israel might also have success with issues of pluralism, social justice, and civil rights. With the encouragement of Rabbi Alexander Schindler, IRAC, the Israel Religious Action Center, a more activist partner of ARZA, came into being with the dynamic Israeli rabbi Uri Regev as its director. Rabbi Regev focused his efforts on matters of religious freedom and the rights of Jews-by-choice in Israel. Because Rabbi Regev is also a lawyer, he was able to bring these cases to Israel's Supreme Court and win them. Suddenly, after years of struggle, these court cases involving the rights of Jews-by-choice, and thereby the rights of the non-Orthodox rabbis in the Diaspora who had converted them, began to capture headlines in Israeli papers.

Rabbi Regev and IRAC raised awareness of Reform Judaism as Israelis read about these victories and the right of the Israel Movement for Progressive Judaism and Reform synagogues in the Jewish State to own land and build progressive institutions. Temple Emanu-El was particularly active in supporting these institutions, especially the Leo Baeck Educational Center in Haifa and Kehilat Mevasseret Tzion in a Jerusalem suburb. ARZA's focus today is to continue to support the Israel Movement for Progressive Judaism financially and to educate American Reform Jews about Israel.

Varied Voices

THE WORLD HAS CHANGED RADICALLY SINCE ISRAEL'S EARLY DAYS. FOR YOUNGER Jews particularly, who cannot remember or conceive of a world without a State of Israel, it is easy to be lulled into apathy and distance. We raised our children to revere pluralism and to condemn injustice. How difficult then to bring into consonance the vision of Israel as a Jewish homeland with the realities of a threatening environment and of a democracy that also preserves the essence of a "Jewish State." These are the challenges facing Temple Emanu-El and the broader Jewish world.

The path to a stronger bond with Israel among American Jews of all ages lies with more in-depth knowledge of each other and the challenges facing both communities. In order to move in these directions and engage in civil discourse on Israel, Temple Emanu-El sponsored "Varied Voices: Building Our Own Voice for Israel," a series of forums about the contemporary challenges facing Israel. Under the leadership of Rabbi Sagal, congregants and community members gather to hear speakers from both sides of the political spectrum, the American Israel Political Action Committee (AIPAC) and J Street, as Temple members engage in dialogue about the issues and dangers facing Israel today. The dialogue continues, as the Temple advances the vital process of education and engagement with the Jewish State.

Commentary

Rabbi Eric H. Yoffie

President Emeritus, Union for Reform Judaism

A FEW YEARS AGO, THE AMERICAN JEWISH COMMUNITY CEASED TO BE THE LARGEST Jewish community in the world. That honor now belongs to the State of Israel. Almost six million of its 7.8 million citizens are Jews.

The Jewish State is cause for rejoicing and thanksgiving. Nothing is more important for the future of the Jewish people than building a vibrant, positive, and productive relationship between the two major centers of Jewish life — the State of Israel and the American Jewish community. This will not be easy. Yes, these two communities are bound by their Jewish identity and their common destiny, but each has created a distinctive, independent Jewish culture. The State of Israel has become a more complex and diverse place than it once was; in many ways, it is more conservative, more nationalist, and more Orthodox, and it is not always easy for American Jews to understand.

But there are ways for American Jews and for individual synagogues and communities to make a connection with Israel. Temple Emanu-El, in building connections with Israel over the last 40 years, has demonstrated how this might be done.

Drawing on Emanu-El's commitment and experience, the following five approaches promote positive engagement of American Jews with Israel.

Person to person connection. In the final analysis, we must remember that Israel is not a cause, it is a place — a place with real people facing real problems, but also looking to connect with Jews around the world. As Birthright has demonstrated, and as Emanu-El has shown, one can talk about Israel forever, but absent personal relationships, ties with the Jewish State will wither. Personal visits to Israel and from Israel are essential.

A strong relationship with the people and institutions of the Israeli Reform Movement. There is much that American Jews do not understand about Israel, and for that reason it is especially important to connect with Israelis who share our values and our devotion to Reform Judaism. Those people are to be found in Israel's Reform Movement, which has begun to take root in Israeli soil. For years, Temple Emanu-El has understood how critical that connection is, and all Reform Jews, following their lead, must develop these ties.

A strong stand for religious freedom and religious pluralism in the Jewish State. Israel is the only place in the Jewish world where Reform rabbis have no legal standing. Due to vigorous advocacy by Israeli Reform Jews, primarily through IRAC, and due to strong support from American congregations such as Temple Emanu-El, this situation is beginning to change. The battle for religious freedom, when conducted in a spirit of love for Israel and commitment to her future, has the potential to inspire and motivate American Reform Jews and to draw them to Israel's side.

Financial support for the State of Israel and for those causes that promote our values. If love of Israel is primarily philanthropy, that love will die. But if our commitment to Israel's future is not expressed in concrete ways, then it is not sincere. Emanu-El has always called on her members to give generously to those programs and projects they see as important, and such support is a key to connection.

Open discussion about Israel's future. Precisely because our emotions about Israel are so strong, it is not always easy in America to have a conversation about difficult and sensitive issues, such as the conflict with the Palestinians, the two-state solution, civil liberties in Israel, and Reform Judaism in Israel. But here too, through programs such as "Varied Voices," Emanu-El has shown the way. Because our love for Israel is unconditional (but not uncritical), we are not afraid to discuss anything, and we know in fact that stifling discussion will only drive the young away.

These, then, are the things we must do to deepen our involvement in the Jewish State. And we do this because we must, because Jewish life cannot be sustained without Israel at its core.

PART IV

Preparing for Our Future

LEARN. PRAY. DO JUSTLY.

CHAPTER ELEVEN

Jewish Education: "It Takes a Congregation"

Helaine Gersten

Temple Emanu-El Religious School Chair, 1978-88

With comments by Rabbi Jan Katzew, PhD

Director of Service Learning, HUC-JIR

Jewish tradition exalts teachers. Ours is the only religious tradition that compares God to a teacher — hamelamed Torah l'amo Yisrael, who is "the Teacher of Torah to the People Israel." If we are in the business of helping people to "enter the Jewish conversation," a conversation that has been going on for 4,000 years, then teachers are the facilitators of that conversation. — Rabbi Sagal

JEWISH EDUCATION IS OFTEN CHARACTERIZED AS AN INSTITUTION IN CRISIS. SUBURBAN children and their parents are pulled in many directions — competitive sports, after-school options, increased homework, and a focus on college entry. Parents who in earlier decades might have volunteered, carpooled, or taught in Religious School work full-time. The Holocaust and the founding of Israel, once motivating factors in Jewish education, no longer resonate for a post-1967 generation. A significant percentage of today's Jewish parents are intermarried.

This crisis may be contemporary, but it is not new. Jewish education has always been supplemental, according to Rabbi Jan Katzew, PhD, director of service learning at HUC-JIR and longtime URJ director of Lifelong Jewish Learning.

The family remains the "primary Jewish educational institution in the Jewish community," he notes. "When the Judaism lived at home is dissonant with the Judaism learned in school, home wins and consequently, too often, Judaism loses."[1] Rabbi Katzew poses the central question for Reform Jewish education: "Accepting the premise that we live in an age defined by choice, how can we raise a generation that will consciously choose to learn and live as Jews?"[2]

At mid-century, when Temple Emanu-El was founded, most Reform Jewish education consisted of a few hours on a Sunday morning with volunteer teachers. A generation later, Jewish education was in decline in many congregations, suffering from fragmentation, lack of funding, and lack of attention.

The American Jewish community was jolted out of its complacency by the 1990 and 2000–01 National Jewish Population Survey, which showed an exponential increase in the rate of intermarriage, reaching 43 percent for those who married between 1985 and 1995.[3]

The crisis in Jewish continuity was real, and the community responded. Over the last two decades, day schools, once primarily Orthodox, spread to every movement. "Religious education" became "lifelong learning" as walls between school and synagogue began to come down. Jewish nursery schools, now called early childhood education, became a key portal into the Jewish community for both children and parents. Attention focused on such informal education opportunities as camping, Israel trips, and youth group. Adult and family education flourished.

As Rabbi Katzew observes, "Reform Jews are becoming more receptive to Jewish distinctiveness. . . . After having succeeded as Americans, it is now a challenge to succeed as Jews."[4]

At the 2001 Biennial, Rabbi Eric Yoffie challenged Reform synagogues to focus on education to transmit Jewish values to succeeding generations:

> Moses understood that while Jews would need an army to defend their
> land, they would need schools to defend their values. And for the next

3,000 years we built our communities around schools. . . . We know that the school cannot succeed on its own — that it needs the active participation of parents. It also needs the commitment of the entire synagogue, which should be an interdependent learning community of which the school is but one part.[5]

Rabbi Katzew calls for a greater focus on collaboration: "We need to cultivate coalitions of Jewish learning among faculty colleagues, parents of our students, education committee members, and congregational leaders. It takes a congregation to rear a Jew."[6]

"And Life is a Journey"

THIS CHAPTER, A RECOUNTING OF JEWISH EDUCATION AT TEMPLE EMANU-EL, IS the story of one such collaboration. It is written as a journey from pre-school through adult bat mitzvah as experienced by the Gersten family.

Each section opens with our family's perspective. I found that our journey is closely intertwined with the evolution of Jewish education and the youth movement, reflecting broader changes in the world at large. I also found that while Temple Emanu-El was not alone in struggling with education issues, we were often ahead of the curve.

Nursery School: "Jewish playgrounds"

WE MOVED TO OUR NEW HOME IN WESTFIELD IN 1972 AND QUICKLY JOINED *Temple Emanu-El. When we expressed interest in the nursery school for our four-year-old daughter Wendy, we were taken to meet its ebullient director, Lisbeth Brodie. On February 7, 1973, Wendy began her first day and Lisbeth Brodie her sixteenth year at Temple Emanu-El's Nursery School.*

The Gersten family's favorite day became Friday when we welcomed Shabbat, chanting blessings over candles, challah, and wine, culminating with services at Temple. We were joined by other nursery school families — all of us delighted by our children's growing Jewish identity.

In 1957, soon after Temple Emanu-El was founded, Sisterhood members Bea Reiss, Betty Barnett, and Dorothy Ehrich had a compelling wish to give their young children a quality Jewish pre-school education. It was a communal effort from Day One. Mothers were on call to help. Fathers built bookcases and shelves still in use today. Rabbi Jack Stern was always poking his head into the classroom.

Lisbeth Brodie, a talented and loving educator, was hired as the first director of the nursery school, where she enjoyed a 25-year career. A survivor who came of age in Poland during the Holocaust, Lisbeth ("Miss Brodie" as she was always known) found a home at Emanu-El where she was "adopted" by many Temple families. Each child who was held in her loving arms and each parent who read her uncannily accurate year-end evaluations owe a debt of gratitude to this remarkable woman.

As times and family needs changed, the school needed to change in order to stay competitive. Ellen Gottdenker and Eileen Eisner instituted enrichment classes and extended the hours. Prescriptive curricula for special education, summer programs, and a continuation of the nurturing methodology of Lisbeth Brodie had parents knocking on our doors once again.

The Emanu-El leadership understood the importance of the formative years. As former youth advisor Brad Gerstle affirmed, "A wise person once said: 'If you want your children to be Jewish adults, you have to give them Jewish playgrounds!'"

This is confirmed by Rabbi Katzew's research. Studying the national issue of today's post–b'nei mitzvah dropouts, he finds that congregations with early childhood programs, where students continue their Jewish education, do better with retention.[7]

From the days of Miss Brodie to the present, Emanu-El has demonstrated its commitment to our youngest students. Today, 170 children are enrolled in Early Childhood Education (ECE). Under the leadership of Director Jill Cimafonte, ECE offers a broad array of class options for children as young as 13 months through a full-day accredited kindergarten program. In addition, LINKS, an ECE young parents group, has proved to be a welcoming home for all families, particularly those in which one parent has little or no Jewish background.

Religious School: Making It a Family Affair

I JOINED THE RELIGIOUS SCHOOL COMMITTEE WITH A VIBRANT GROUP OF PARENTS EAGER *to "give back" and help provide the best Jewish educational experience for the students at Temple Emanu-El. In 1978 I became Religious School committee chair, a post I held for 10 years.*

Sisterhood provided funding and oversight for the Religious School beginning in 1955. Bea Reiss recalls, "We were a warm, committed nucleus and very proud. We were aware that as parents we must set examples so that our children, the next generation, would learn from us. We also understood that many of us were uneducated about Reform Jewish customs, and so we learned alongside our children."

The 1960s: Social and Ethical Concerns

THE NATION'S FEELINGS OF ANXIETY AND FEAR AFTER THE ASSASSINATIONS OF President John F. Kennedy and other public figures, the looming Vietnam War and the social upheaval in its wake, proved deeply challenging, especially to young people.

Under the leadership of Principal Lillian Adler, Temple Emanu-El set up an innovative program for ninth graders, with Temple members presenting lectures on topics of world concern and the Jewish response to moral and ethical issues. The primary goal was to help students and parents recognize the importance of working together as a *kehillah* (community).

In the mid-1960s Religious School requirements were strengthened. B'nei mitzvah increased, and Confirmation was extended to tenth grade, with the number of confirmands reaching as many as 65 or more per year. The most popular class by far was Rabbi Kroloff's seminar, "The Jewish View of Sex, Love, and Marriage."

The 1970s: Creating a "Culture of Expectation"

As part of his prescription for retention of Jewish students, Rabbi Katzew calls for creating a synagogue-wide "culture of expectation, clearly indicating from the outset that Jewish learning lies at the heart of our identity; it is our very essence."[8]

Rabbi Howard "Hesh" Sommer, hired as both assistant rabbi and director of education in 1977, felt strongly about this comprehensive approach to Jewish education. "If children aren't excited about Jewish learning and parents aren't involved, there can be no future for Judaism. Our task must be to involve the entire family in a more exciting form of Judaic learning, involving partnerships with teachers and the clergy."

Family weekend retreats were introduced along with courses on comparative religion and other contemporary issues. Learning became intergenerational, as students interviewed grandparents for an Ellis Island Simulation experience. Reflecting the increasing importance of education in the synagogue, Religious School chair became a Temple board position.

This new emphasis aligns with Rabbi Katzew's finding that "congregations that offer ongoing family education programs and retreats have higher retention rates. In these synagogues, the focus is on the family, not the individual student, enabling parents to model for their children the idea of lifelong Jewish learning."[9]

Rabbi Sommer, as well as other rabbis and educators who followed, stressed another key factor, the role of parents. In synagogues where students stayed on past their b'nei mitzvah, Rabbi Katzew finds, "parents overwhelmingly indicate that they either required or strongly encouraged their children" to continue.[10]

Another key finding was that congregations showing high student retention rates have a significant percentage of parents who were *not* raised as Jews. Katzew observes that, although it may seem counterintuitive, "when parents have made a decision to raise their children as Jews, they see their children's Jewish education as a sacred lifelong commitment."[11]

The 1980s: Social Upheaval, Inspirational Leadership

THE DECADE OF THE '80s USHERED IN GREAT SOCIAL AND ECONOMIC CHANGE, AS CIVIL discontent and violence in the Middle East enveloped us, and economic inequality became an issue. During this era, Temple Emanu-El also became part of the sad but growing percentage of communities experiencing family separations and divorce.

In 1982 Helga Newmark, a child survivor of the Holocaust, became director of education. She brought to the post an incomparable wisdom, sensitivity, moral commitment, and inner strength that gave purpose and heart to Jewish learning.

Helga, through her experience of suffering and loss, found meaning in educating others, "so that my life and others' are not lived in vain." A writer and poet, Helga could, as she said, "look at life through the eyes of a child, yet communicate as an adult."

Helga's depth of understanding, compassion, and spiritual leadership were precisely what was needed in this troubled era.

Postscript: Helga served as education director until 1989. At the age of 58, she was accepted into the HUC-JIR Rabbinic Studies program and received a standing ovation at her ordination. Friends and colleagues mourned her death in 2012.

The 1990s: Peer Leadership, *Tzedakah,* Israel

IN 1989 TEMPLE EMANU-EL WELCOMED TAMARA COTY (NOW TAMARA RUBEN) AS THE next director of education. Tamara, an educator and an Iraqi Jew raised in Israel, brought a heightened professionalism to the school and raised the level of Hebrew literacy.

Partnering with Assistant Rabbi Marc Disick, Tamara co-created, designed, and implemented the highly popular *Gesher L'Kesher* (Bridge to Connections) Peer Leadership program for eighth to twelfth grade students, which continues to this day. Yvette Golum was the program's first adult leader, overseeing the teaching process, training, and post-class debriefing.

The decade of the '90s also ushered in a time of "irrational exuberance" as markets soared and people became wealthy overnight. Tamara felt it was important to give a moral focus to material wealth through *tzedakah* (charity). Encouraging thoughtful discussions, conversations with visiting speakers, and the importance of caring, giving, and receiving, she led each class to discuss and vote on "our charity of the week." Some weeks the Keren Ami Fund received as much as $1,000.

Tamara was also intent on creating greater interest in Israel. She initiated a two-year grant program, *ANI V'ATAH* (You & I), matching Emanu-El with a synagogue in the Israeli town of Arad. Several Temple Emanu-El students traveled to Israel for a two-week visit, staying with the families of their new Israeli friends. The following year, we played host to our Israeli counterparts.

Parents Toby Ganz and Leslie Glickstein sought a program devoted to children with special needs. The Ma'ayan program, beginning with four children, was initiated as a self-contained, holiday-based program filled with song, art, and fun. Outreach with the Jewish Federation of Greater MetroWest's Autism/Asperger's program was instrumental to its success.

Education Today: Engaging Teens and Families

THE RELIGIOUS SCHOOL CONTINUES TO THRIVE, FIRST WITH DIRECTOR OF Education David Gronlund-Jacob and currently with Abra Lee.

Music, always an important component of Jewish education at Emanu-El, gained new emphasis with the appointment of Cantor Michelle Rubel in 2012. A former student of Cantor Novick, she focuses on music for school and youth programs.

Engaging families remains critical. Emanu-El's Family Education program starts early, involving primary grade parents as together they create "toolkits" for bringing Shabbat into the home.

Bar and bat mitzvah are critical milestones in Jewish family life. Cantor Martha Novick, who directs the b'nei mitzvah program, understands the many pressures and competing interests for today's children and their parents and tries to meet families where they are.

Meeting the Post–B'nei Mitzvah Challenge

Emanu-El clergy and educators are working in concert to keep post–b'nei mitzvah students engaged in Jewish experience with several innovative formal and informal programs geared to their changing needs and interests.

- Tuesday night school has been renamed *HaMakom* ("The Place"), with the rabbis as lead teachers. *HaMakom* is a two-hour experience for seventh, eighth, and ninth graders, combining study with visits to places outside Temple walls, such as the Community Foodbank, New Jersey's inner cities, and Philadelphia's historic Jewish centers.

- The tenth grade Confirmation program is designed to help students build community with one another, wrestle with important issues of the day, express their beliefs as Jewish young adults, and engage in *tikkun olam*.

- Under the direction of lay leader Steve Natko and the rabbis, *Gesher L'Kesher* continues to play a major role in helping Emanu-El teens learn leadership skills and form strong bonds with each other. Juniors and seniors study challenging issues from a Jewish perspective for three months and then mentor seventh, eighth, and ninth graders on these issues, forming relationships and creating a "safe" community for discussion, friendship, and support.

- Older students visit campuses to sample college life and explore what it means to be Jewish once they leave Emanu-El.

- High school juniors and seniors are invited to meet with Rabbi Sagal and Rabbi Glazer at "Café Torah," Sunday evening gatherings at the Westfield Diner for informal discussions of issues that matter.

- Cantor Novick's popular trips to hurricane-devastated New Orleans with eleventh and twelfth graders, together with Emanu-El building superintendent Mike

Kenny, focus on the important lessons of learning and social justice. "Watching their eyes open wide and hearing them say: 'I can make a difference' is a joy to behold," she says.

Adult Education: Advancing the "Jewish conversation" among Adults

IN 1955 THE ADULT EDUCATION COMMITTEE WAS FORMED AND A GOLDEN AGE OF adult education began at Temple Emanu-El. Rabbi Stern initiated the Tuesday morning Bible Class, one of the longest-running uninterrupted adult study programs of its kind in the Reform Movement.

When Rabbi Kroloff came to Temple Emanu-El in 1966, he appointed Harold Wasserman as Adult Education chairman, ushering in a second golden age of education and drawing large crowds who wanted to learn from outstanding Jewish scholars and thinkers. There were Hebrew classes teaching prayer book literacy and *ulpan* classes in conversational Hebrew for congregants planning to travel to Israel. Noted scholars included Harry Orlinsky, Steve Berk, W. Gunther Plaut, Eugene Borowitz, Lawrence Hoffman, Harold Kushner, Norman Lamm, Richard Rubenstein, Howard Sacher, Norman Cohen, and Robert Bull. Elie Wiesel spoke to overflow audiences on five occasions.

Today's offerings have shifted from "star" speakers to programs that respond to this generation's needs and interests. More than 20 adult education classes are offered. Sessions focus on spirituality, community, and "hands-on" Judaism, together with traditional study of Jewish text and history geared to all levels of knowledge and backgrounds, Jewish and non-Jewish.

The Tuesday morning Bible class remains the centerpiece. Executive Director Carolyn Shane notes, "The class is continually packed with adults eager to learn and share ideas, with weekly attendance reaching 70 strong and over. I constantly hear our members say, 'I never knew that learning could be so exciting and so much fun.'"

We are blessed to have Rabbi Eric Yoffie as a member of Emanu-El. Rabbi Sagal notes: "I will always regard Rabbi Yoffie's embrace of Torah learning as the responsibility of every Reform Jew as his greatest contribution. One cannot enter a Reform congregation without seeing serious learning taking place. Rabbi Yoffie's High Holy Day presentations at Emanu-El remain 'sold out.'"

Adult Bar/Bat Mitzvah: "Jewish learning enables us to become more substantial human beings."

Fon ME, ADULT BAR/BAT MITZVAH PROVED TO BE THE ULTIMATE ADULT EDUCATION *experience at Temple Emanu-El. As a child reared in the Orthodox tradition, I had never been a bat mitzvah. Finally, in 1998, I began my studies. My bat mitzvah in 1999 was the culmination of a journey I began when the Gersten family joined Temple Emanu-El in 1972, and I found my own voice in Reform Judaism. I captured highlights of this profound experience with each teacher in my journal. Here is a brief sampling:*

> Year One: *Rabbi Zamore.* For me, this journey is a gift long-delayed. . . .
> *Rabbi Kroloff.* Reading *Jewish Literacy* is becoming an important part of
> my daily activities. . . . *Cantor Novick.* Her lyrical, magic voice encourages
> us to share our stories. . . . *Rabbi Goldberg.* I am touched by my fellow stu-
> dents. What a great opportunity to connect to the "Jewish Counselors" in
> Torah. . . . *Rabbi Gluck.* We discuss why we study the same book over and
> over. *It* doesn't change, *we* do . . . we are the wave, God is the ocean. . . .
> *Tamara Coty.* Prayer is a blessing, a blame, a reason, a strength, embracer,
> peace, tranquility.
>
> Year Two finds us deep in study, chanting, speech, butterflies. Fi-
> nally I stand at the podium on the *bimah*, sharing in the affirmations of our
> faith as I reach this joyous moment and become bat mitzvah.

Rabbi Kroloff relates a conversation with a recent graduate of the adult b'nei mitzvah program who said his Jewish studies literally transformed his life. This experience can extend to all Emanu-El education offerings, from pre-school through adult. "Studying Jewish ethics and values helps us make decisions all through our personal and professional lives," the rabbi observes. "Jewish learning enables us to become more substantial human beings."

Commentary

Rabbi Douglas Sagal
Temple Emanu-El Senior Rabbi

L ET ME SAY IT CATEGORICALLY: THERE IS NOTHING, *NOTHING* MORE IMPORTANT than creating a vibrant home at Temple Emanu-El for children and young people. The old view of Jewish education for the young as some kind of "painful experience to be endured" is as outdated as the mechanical typewriter and the eight-track tape.

One of the strengths of Emanu-El is our willingness to evaluate, re-evaluate, and evaluate again every aspect of our educational programming. We will never be entirely satisfied and never feel that we have reached "perfection" in our quest to create a vibrant, stimulating, *transformational* educational program that is suffused with *joy*.

Some thoughts for the future of education at Emanu-El:

1. Future education will be centered on reaching every child as an individual. We reject the "one size fits all" model and will strive to identify the appropriate learning style for every one of our students.

2. We know that much depends on relationships. What happens between the teacher and the student or the clergy and the student in terms of their relationship is just as important as the information that is imparted. The relationship between teacher and *talmid* (student) is critical.

3. We will challenge students to direct their own learning. We will encourage students to find friends, assemble a group, and tell us what *they* want to learn. Get a group together. We will get you a teacher.

4. More and more resources will go to learning. Learning has been the key to Jewish life for four thousand years. Moses Maimonides depicts Abraham as a teacher. The prophet Moses is called "Moses our Teacher." Even God is "Teacher of Torah to the People Israel." More and more of the precious resources of our Temple will go to teaching both children and adults.

Chapter Notes

1. Rabbi Jan Katzew, "CHAI — Learning for Jewish Life," *Agenda: Jewish Education,* Jewish Education Service of North America (JESNA), Vol. 15, 35. Summer 2002. http://www.bjpa.org/Publications/details.cfm?PublicationID=958.

2. Ibid.

3. "The National Jewish Population Survey 2000–01: Strength, Challenge and Diversity in the American Jewish Population." A United Jewish Communities Report in Cooperation with the Mandell L. Berman Institute — North American Jewish Data Bank, September 2003, updated January 2004, 16. http://www.jewishfederations.org/local_includes/downloads/4606.pdf

4. Katzew, "A Reformation in Jewish Education," *The Ultimate Jewish Teacher's Handbook,* Nachama Skolnik Moskowitz, ed. (Springfield, N.J.: A.R.E. Publishing, Inc. 2003), 38-39.

5. Quoted in Katzew, "CHAI," 36.

6. Katzew, "Reformation," 35.

7. "Education: Preventing Post B'nai Mitzvah Dropout-itis," A Conversation with Rabbi Jan Katzew, *Reform Judaism Magazine,* Winter 2009. http://reformjudaismmag.org/Articles/index.cfm?id=1538

8. Ibid.

9. Ibid.

10. Ibid.

11. Ibid.

CHAPTER TWELVE

Youth Engagement: Creating "On-Ramps" to the Jewish Future

Helaine Gersten

Temple Emanu-El Religious School Chair, 1978-88

This chapter recaps the life- and movement-changing impact of the Reform Jewish youth orga-nization, Temple Emanu-El's and our own family's experience, and a forward look at the new URJ Campaign for Youth Engagement.

The First Sixty Years: "And the dreamer keeps a-dreamin' ages long"

THE DEVELOPMENT OF TODAY'S REFORM JEWISH LEADERSHIP IS CLOSELY INTERTWINED with the history of NFTY, the North American Federation of Temple Youth. Countless rabbis, cantors, teachers, and congregational and community leaders were nurtured by this remarkable organization and, in turn, nurtured generations that followed.

While the founding of NFTY dates back to 1939, the organization took hold in the 1940s and 1950s under the leadership of Rabbi Sam Cook. As Rabbi Jerome Davidson, rabbi emeritus of Temple Beth-El, Great Neck, New York, past NFTY national president and member of the HUC-JIR faculty and board of governors, re-calls, "Sam transformed NFTY . . . from a federation of youth groups to a revolu-tionary new Jewish experience for teenagers."[1]

NFTY brought young people together in camp settings "not only for educating the minds of youth but also charging their emotions with a love of Jewish living." Rabbi Cook had two essential policies, according to Rabbi Davidson. "He encouraged the participation of rabbis especially attuned to the needs and feelings of young people" and "insisted on empowering the young people themselves by giving them the responsibility of developing their own activities within the camp, their adult mentors guiding but not directing them."[2]

Eleanor (Ellie) Schwartz, longtime NFTY associate director and later NFTS executive director, describes how the NFTY experience impacted not only a generation of young Reform Jews but also their home congregations as well. Young people who attended camp leadership institutes at places like Olin Sang Ruby Union Institute in Oconomowoc, Wisconsin, Camp Swig in Santa Rosa, California, and Kutz Camp in Warwick, New York, "returned home to hundreds of congregations and communities in North America transformed by the discovery of their own talents and abilities, proud of skills learned, eager to share with their own groups, pleased with new friends and new horizons."[3] They brought the energy, spirit, and music of these experiences home, challenging their congregations to reinvigorate American Jewish life.

Building on this foundation, NFTY introduced innovative new programs such as Mitzvah Corps, where students live and work in inner cities in the United States, Israel, Puerto Rico, and Mexico for a summer; Torah Corps, giving young people an opportunity to study and have fun together in an informal camp setting; the Eisendrath International Exchange (EIE) program for North American and Israeli youth; and NFTY Israel trips, now expanded to include a special Reform Jewish Birthright experience for young adults.

The music introduced in camps, conclaves, national institutes, and everywhere NFTY gathered has transformed Temple Emanu-El and other Reform Jewish congregations, introducing a spirited, contemporary style and injecting a new energy into Shabbat services. Rabbi Allan ("Smitty") Smith, former director of the UAHC Youth Division, recalls that by the end of the 1970s "NFTY song leaders were composing music with which to pray and play. . . . Debbie Friedman, Jeff Klepper, and Dan Freelander, Ramie and Merri Arian, and, of course, [Jeff and Danny's popular singing group] Kol B'Seder performed throughout the land of NFTY."[4]

The focus on youth also inspired Reform Jewish camping. The first URJ camp opened in 1951 in Oconomowoc, growing into a vibrant network of 13 camps throughout the country, many of which sponsor Israel trips.

NFTY awakened young people to social justice issues, advocating over the years for American farm workers, Soviet and Ethiopian Jewry, women's reproductive rights, civil rights for African-Americans and for gays and lesbians. Field trips to the URJ Religious Action Center in Washington continue to offer generations of young people a way to express their commitment to social justice in a Jewish context.

One of the great and lasting values of NFTY and other youth programs has been young people's exposure to others beyond the borders of their small towns, cities, and suburbs. They come to understand the differing lifestyles and values of both their peers and the people they help. Perhaps most valuable, the teens come into contact with inspiring adults, role models who teach by example that being Jewish is not only exciting, fun, and intellectually and spiritually meaningful, but also can help change the world.

Temple Emanu-El Youth Group: TEWTY, making Judaism "cool and fun" while developing the next generation of Jewish leaders

H*OW WELL MARV AND I REMEMBER THE CLASS RABBI KROLOFF AND HIS WIFE TERRY presented to parents of children approaching their bar/bat mitzvah year. Rabbi Kroloff counseled: "One day soon you will say goodnight to your son/daughter and the next morning you will say good morning to someone you have never seen before." Terry said, "You will survive. Rearrange your priorities, pray a lot, and talk to one another. Oh, and INSIST they join Youth Group. You'll need all the help you can get."*

1955 marked the formation of "Temple Emanu-El of Westfield Temple Youth," or TEWTY, our first youth group. Jewish identity, involvement in social action projects, and an understanding of the Jewish tradition to reach out and help others were of paramount importance in its creation.

Rabbi Lennard Thal ushered in the decade of the '70s as the first professional youth director. Soon programs such as the Soviet Jewry candlelight march down East Broad Street with Torah scrolls integrated our youth in a dynamic, relevant way into the life of the Temple. Lenny was the first of many Hebrew Union College student rabbis who transformed the senior youth program into one of the strongest in the state. Rabbis Arnold Gluck, Joel Soffin, Marc Disick, and other assistant rabbis followed, contributing their own brand of charisma and commitment, making a deep impact on the teenagers with whom they worked.

Parents are critical factors in the equation as Brad Gerstle, who led the youth group in 2007, points out. "Students really need parental support in order to make their youth group experience a priority during these important adolescent years," he advises. Brad worked with an expanded youth program, including Chaverim for third to fifth grades, Kadima for sixth to eighth grades, and TEWTY for high school.

Some of the best settings for encouraging young people to stay connected to Jewish life are the URJ summer camps. While a number of Emanu-El youngsters attend Eisner and Crane Lake camps, and those of high school age go to Kutz Camp, Emanu-El has a special relationship with Camp Harlam in Pennsylvania. During the summer, Rabbis Sagal and Smiley spend time in residence, and fifth, sixth, and seventh graders go there on retreats during the school year.

Another important touchstone for Emanu-El young people has been JFTY, Jersey Federation of Temple Youth, now known as NFTY-GER (Garden Empire Region). TEWTY members are able to expand their horizons by attending regional and national conventions, conclaves, institutes, and specialized programs such as Urban Mitzvah Corps. They engage with their peers and with people they might never otherwise encounter, learn from and bond with charismatic Jewish adults, and gain hands-on leadership training by taking on local, regional, and national responsibilities.

To this day, countless graduates of URJ camps and Temple Emanu-El's youth programs point to these experiences as transformational events that directed them onto new, life-changing paths. Inspired by their NFTY camping, Mitzvah Corps, Israel, and youth group experiences, they have gone on to direct social justice organizations, train to become rabbis, cantors, and educators, and serve as volunteers and officers in hundreds of synagogues across North America. Some of them — now in their 40s, 50s, and even 60s — still count their TEWTY and JFTY pals among their closest friends.

Many of our children still speak about their youth group leaders' lasting influence. Our daughter Wendy vividly recalls, "Rabbi Arnie Gluck brought Judaism out of the classroom and truly 'to life' for all of us." The impact of those early years continues. Wendy has worked as a lay leader and a professional in the Boston Jewish community and non-profits for 20 years.

Today, however, youth engagement in Jewish life across nearly all denominations is at risk. Emanu-El is taking steps to change that dynamic. For example, Rabbi Erin Glazer has introduced a national program aimed at sixth grade girls entitled "*Rosh Chodesh:* It's a Girl Thing!" Part of Moving Traditions, a national movement aimed at deeper engagement with Judaism, the program is designed to deal with post–bat mitzvah dropout and the loss of self-esteem in young women as they enter adolescence. The *Rosh Chodesh* program draws on Jewish teachings and traditions to keep girls healthy and Jewish, despite the aspects of popular culture that encourage risky behaviors. The goal, according to Rabbi Glazer, is to "help girls see Judaism as a resource to help them navigate their adolescent and teen years." A related program for eighth and ninth grade boys, "*Shevet Achim*: The Brotherhood," was introduced in 2012 and is currently led by Rabbi Joshua Leighton.

Shifting the Focus to Relationships and Community: "Provide for yourself a teacher; get yourself a friend; judge every [person] towards merit."

We are at a crossroads. Our Jewish communities are full of dedicated and creative lay people and professionals who successfully engage many youth and families. And yet research tells us that if current trends continue in our congregations, approximately 80 percent of the children who become b'nei mitzvah will have no connection of any kind to their synagogue by the time they reach twelfth grade. And even fewer will live their lives as actively engaged Jews.

URJ Campaign for Youth Engagement — A Call to Action[5]

The landscape for youth involvement has changed radically since the early years. Young people have other priorities. Parents are stressed by multiple demands on their time, energy, and finances; raising teens is as challenging as ever. Financially stressed synagogues allocate less money for youth activities. It's not surprising that so many youth programs are running on empty.

Recognizing the dimensions of the challenge, the URJ determined to reverse the direction, making bar and bat mitzvah an "on-ramp" to further Jewish engagement rather than an "off-ramp" from Jewish life and practice. At the 2011 Biennial, Rabbi Jonah Pesner, URJ senior vice president, presented the Campaign for Youth Engagement Call to Action as a top priority, challenging the URJ and congregations to make the commitment personal.

Campaign leaders conducted "1,000 grassroots conversations" with teens, parents, grandparents, educators, rabbis, youth workers, cantors, administrators, lay leaders, and URJ professionals at all levels to find out what engages teens. The conclusion: "Building meaningful *relationships* and a dynamic and engaged Jewish *community* is essential for youth and their families to commit to Jewish life."

Rabbi Michael White, senior rabbi at Temple Sinai, Roslyn Heights, New York, and an early champion of this effort, says, "There is something special about connecting to a community where you are embraced and accepted. Kids today *crave* a place where they're not judged on shallow externals but challenged on moral terms. It's less about program and more about creating contexts where relationships with peers and mentors can develop and flourish."

The URJ has committed to:

- Retraining youth professionals. Successful youth engagement depends on the consistent presence of caring, talented, well-trained individuals who make Judaism come to life for youth and families.

- Expanding opportunities for affordable, accessible "immersive" experiences such as camping, Israel trips, and service projects.

- Engaging young Jewish adults in their 20s and 30s, outside the synagogue if need be, to help them connect to Judaism before they marry and have children.

- Changing the culture of synagogue life to focus attention and resources on youth.

The Reform Movement is tackling a key challenge — navigating the many transitions in Jewish life, bridging from one stage to the next, and working across programs and institutions to foster connections. Throughout this effort, parent engagement is seen as critical.

While there is much to be done, Temple Emanu-El actively seeks to incorporate these key principles of mentoring, community, acceptance, and values. Rabbi Sarah Smiley, who is responsible for youth programming at Emanu-El, said, "In *Pirkei Avot* we learn 'Provide for yourself a teacher; get yourself a friend; and judge every [person] towards merit.' These three qualities permeate our youth groups. We try to insert Judaism into every event in an environment where all participants feel safe sharing their opinions and learning new things."

Rabbi Smiley is encouraged by the resources URJ is committing to youth engagement nationally. A new Reform Youth Professionals Association brings together rabbis, cantors, educators, and others trained in working with young people, underscoring the value of youth work and its role in the future of Jewish life.

Closer to home, Rabbi Smiley is impressed by Temple Emanu-El's leadership in all aspects of education, from the lively pre-school program to the vitality and popularity of the Tuesday morning adult Bible class: "Emanu-El truly lives *l'dor v'dor*, transmitting Jewish learning and values from generation to generation."

It is now 40 years since Marv and I have been blessed to be members of Temple Emanu-El's family. Our Jewish identity and religious traditions have been strengthened and passed down l'dor v'dor *to our daughter Wendy and her sons, Will and Sam, our precious grandsons. The boys' lives are enriched by their mother's deep commitment to her family's Temple life.*

Rabbi Tarfon's wisdom has been a constant in our lives: "It is not incumbent upon you to complete the task, but neither are you free to desist from it altogether."

Your Temple Emanu-El family awaits. You have but to open its doors to feed your mind and soul.

Chapter Notes

1. Rabbi Jerome K. Davidson, "A Tribute to Rabbi Sam Cook," *NFTYology: Past, Present, Future; Ani v'Atah*, The Newsletter of the North American Federation of Temple Youth, NFTY Convention Edition, February 2005, 2. http://www.nfty. org/_kd/Items/actions.cfm?action=Show&item_id=730&destination=ShowItem

2. Ibid.

3. Eleanor Schwartz, "The NFTY 50's," *NFTYology*, 11.

4. Rabbi Allan Smith, "The NFTY 70's," *NFTYology*, 13.

5. URJ Campaign for Youth Engagement Call to Action: http://urj.org/kd/_temp/8A111A29-1D09-6781-A19DC278BC44E041/Call%20to%20Action%20Executive%20Summary.web.pdf

CHAPTER THIRTEEN

"It's Not Your Grandma's Judaism": Temple as an Inclusive Community

Rabbi Charles A. Kroloff
Temple Emanu-El Rabbi Emeritus

Accor ding to my family's oral history, my great-great-grandfather owned a tavern in the Jewish Pale of Russia. One day Russian Cossack soldiers burst into the tavern, demanded drink for all, and then slaughtered him, his wife, and one of his daughters.

It's clear that Judaism in Westfield is not our ancestors' nineteenth-century Jewish *shtetl*. Every moment of every day their physical survival was on the line. They confronted military conscription and endemic anti-Semitism. They faced a bleak future.

Nor is it my grandfather's Judaism. He was one of many Kroloff relatives, peddlers who migrated west from New York's Lower East Side, who eventually set up shop in Sioux City, Iowa. They created supportive family enclaves, not quite a transplanted *shtetl*, but a solid family structure that embraced them as they faced the challenges of a strange culture and an unforgiving economy.

Nor does our Judaism resemble my mother's in Atlanta. Growing up, as she did, in the shadow of the Ku Klux Klan lynching of the Jewish businessman Leo Frank, she enjoyed a comfortable childhood that placed a high premium on self-conscious assimilation into the Southern ethos.

Like many of my contemporaries, I grew up shaped by the destruction of European Jewry, the establishment of the Jewish State, and the prophetic mandate that we Jews were expected to feed the hungry and free the oppressed. Mine has been a world in which Jews have become more secure, assuming leadership in every sector of American life.

For the last 40 years, Jews, like most Americans, have been on the move. One out of every five Americans moves every year. Never before in history have so many people lived alone. Never before have families been so geographically dispersed, and never before have families been so small. We intermarry at the rate of 45 percent. We join synagogues later and leave them earlier than our ancestors did. Our ties to Israel are weaker than they have been in 55 years.

In the mid-1950s, when Temple Emanu-El was founded, the move to the suburbs was on and synagogue membership was exploding, no matter what anyone did. What is it they were seeking? Community.

HUC-JIR professor Rabbi Larry Hoffman reminds us that "once upon a time, in the villages that made up America, pretty much everyone was part of a natural community consisting of a few hundred souls, organized around a central church (for us, a synagogue)," that people could easily walk to. Like the general store, a place where people gathered to get the news, exchange gossip, and leave messages.

What the general store was for farmers, the synagogue was for Jews — the taken-for-granted social centerpiece of their lives. Everyone joined, and, sometimes, everyone showed up. The scene evokes the old Jewish joke: Schwartz says, "I don't go to *shul* to talk to God. But my friend Klein, he goes there to talk to God, and I go there to talk to Klein."

When I was studying to be a rabbi, I served a student pulpit in Fairmont, West Virginia. One evening, I had Shabbat dinner with a longtime congregant — let's call him "Schwartz." After supper, we walked together to *shul*. On the way, Schwartz disclosed that he didn't believe in God. Naively I asked, "So why are you going to synagogue tonight?" He gave me his answer in a heartbeat: "Because I need to be with other Jews."

Community today, be it Facebook, Twitter, or synagogues (and there is a difference, I hope), is an attempt to recover the lost sense of belonging that used to come from natural groupings like the general store. Community is a place where we find relationships that support us and nurture us. I randomly checked the websites of 20 Reform and Conservative synagogues throughout America. Sixteen described themselves as a "warm" or a "caring community."

What is happening within these caring, religious communities?

For one thing, all kinds of healing is taking place. I cannot begin to count the number of people who have told me over the years how much comfort they received when they were observing *shiva* and their fellow congregants showed up. The mourner may not have known them or spoken to them. Their sheer presence at a time of vulnerability and pain brought them connection and assurance that, yes, they would move beyond their loss, they would see a better day.

For several years after my retirement, I consulted and led services at Fairmount Temple in Cleveland. During the afternoon of Yom Kippur, I invited anyone who wished to ascend the *bimah* and spend some moments of meditation before the open ark. One woman who came up had been struggling with cancer for years. She told me later that this was the most powerful moment of healing she had ever experienced. At that instant, all of us, whether we remained in our seats, stood silently, or ascended the *bimah*, had created a sacred community for that woman and for each other.

Today, Temple Emanu-El is just such a community:

- A community that says: no Jew should ever be alone during times of illness, loss, or difficult transition.

- A community that says: bring us the deepest concerns of your soul and the soaring aspirations of your spirit.

- A community that says: share with us your own personal narrative and we will hear you; *Mah sheyotzei min halev nichnas el halev*, that which flows from the heart will enter the heart.

- A community that says: you will always be accepted here, not because of status or reputation, but for who you are and for the search that you are on.

In this community our *simchas* are deepened and our souls enriched because they are shared. On a memorable Friday night, decades ago, a man who had studied for conversion with me stood on the *bimah* to be welcomed into our faith. The ceremony was lovely, but the memorable part occurred when he walked off the pulpit and entered the center aisle. At that point, the congregation spontaneously poured out of the pews to embrace him, to hug him, to rejoice with him. And the tears flowed from a community that had transformed another human being and was transformed by him.

To paraphrase Rabbi Larry Kushner, "Organized religion may have its problems, but it is light years ahead of doing it all alone."

This is not our grandmas' Judaism. But it is ours — to make it what we want it to be. We must listen to the voices of those who are searching, especially the young Jews who affiliate later than their parents, but who are no less in search of a life of the spirit. To the surprise of many of us, younger Jews are more inclined than their parents to talk about God.

They love music, especially if it is participatory and personally engaging. One large synagogue in New England abandoned its traditional liturgy, handed out percussion, and guess what? Jews under 35, whom they had never seen before, showed up to pray. Temple Emanu-El's Shabbat Hallelu, initiated by Cantor Novick, offers a solid foundation for the renewal of prayer. I will never forget seeing a young mother during Hallelu. Her eyes were closed, her arms wrapped around her four-year-old child, her body tilting slowly left and right, her spirit engaged in the pure ecstasy of Shabbat celebration.

Something else very important is happening in the community that American Jews are creating. Most of us are more interested in whom we can INCLUDE and less interested in whom we can EXCLUDE. Marriage between two Jews is still a priority for the Jewish people and for me. And yet, the intermarried are among the most spiritual members of our Jewish community today.

When I met with my class of second-year rabbinic students at HUC-JIR a few years ago, I asked them to share their backgrounds. Nearly half the class had grown up with one non-Jewish parent or was herself or himself a Jew-by-choice. This was not my rabbinic class, nor was it Rabbi Sagal's. Not even Rabbi Glazer's. That's how fast Judaism is changing.

I am especially grateful to the mothers and fathers at Temple Emanu-El who are not Jewish, but who are an integral part of a Jewish family. Many have created a Jewish home, or carpool to Temple, or pray or study at Emanu-El. I want to honor and express appreciation to these people for raising Jewish children and bringing their own unique strength to the inclusive Jewish community emerging in America. INclusion trumps EXclusion.

In 2009, Alyssa Stanton became a rabbi, the first African-American to be ordained by a mainstream Jewish seminary. When HUC-JIR ordained her, we declared: "Our doors are open wide to the representatives of this new America." When the 60 white families of Temple Bayt Shalom in Greenville, North Carolina, invited her to be their rabbi, they declared: "This is not our grandmas' Judaism, or even our grandmas' Old South." Our strength is in diversity; our future will be built on inclusion.

Inclusion has been at the foundation of our tradition since the time of Moses. After 40 years in the wilderness, Moses gathers the people of Israel and proclaims: *Atem nitzavim hayom kul'chem lifney Adonai, Eloheichem, rosheichem, shivteichem, zikneichem, v'shotreichem, kol ish Yisrael.* "You are standing here this day, all of you, before Adonai, your God, the heads of your tribes, your elders, your children and wives, even the stranger in your camp, from the chopper of wood to the drawer of water, that you may enter into the Covenant God has established with us."

What the Torah teaches is that not one person in the congregation may be shunted to the margins of this community. All are at the center. As I read Torah, the Covenant is a big tent. It includes old, young, and middle-aged, poor and rich, women and men, dark-skinned and lighter, straight and gay, believers, atheists, agnostics, and non-Jews who belong to our families, and many more.

We Jews need all the strength we can muster. That is why Reform Judaism has opened its doors wide to those who have been disenfranchised for so long. Women become rabbis, cantors, and synagogue presidents. Gays and lesbians discover doors open wide. Jews with special needs find a spiritual home.

Most of the American Jewish community has criticized Reform Judaism for emphasizing inclusion over exclusion. But note that within 10 years of each bold decision, every branch of American Judaism except the Orthodox has followed our example. I point this out not to be triumphalist, nor to argue that we are better Jews. Far from it. I emphasize this simply to demonstrate that inclusion is THE clear, persistent, and inspiring trend in our community.

If the Jewish people is to grow and prosper, our Covenant, like the one God made with Israel at Sinai, must embrace a broad community. And we must offer that community nothing less than a joyful song, an outstretched hand, and a soaring spirit.

CHAPTER FOURTEEN

"Keep Climbing the Mountain"

Rabbi Douglas Sagal

Temple Emanu-El Senior Rabbi

Rabbi Sagal was the featured speaker for Westfield's 2014 Martin Luther King Day observance, hosted by Temple Emanu-El. His remarks bring together the many themes of this book and give eloquent voice to the dreams that began with the founders of Temple Emanu-El and continue to this day: a decades-long commitment to learning, praying, and doing justly.

IN OBSERVANCE OF MARTIN LUTHER KING DAY, RABBI SMILEY, CANTOR NOVICK, and Mike Kenny, our building supervisor, are with 20 of our local high school students in the Ninth Ward in New Orleans, spending this weekend remembering Dr. King by working to restore homes in that still ravaged area. They are also engaged in fellowship with a number of New Orleans churches with whom we have built a relationship. This is the seventh year in a row that students from Temple Emanu-El have chosen to spend the King weekend in New Orleans, and we are justifiably proud of them and the work they are doing in memory of Dr. King.

In the synagogue, we are currently reading from the Book of Exodus, specifically the portion that deals with Moses' ascent to the top of Mount Sinai. Moses, accompanied by his servant, Joshua, ascends the mountain. The people gathered at the foot of the mountain are granted the awesome privilege of hearing the voice of the Lord, as God proclaims the commandments to all humanity. That's right as the

Jewish tradition sees it. The commandments spoken by God are available for all humanity, not just the ancient Israelites at the foot of the mountain. The Bible simply says, "And God spoke all these words." The Ten Commandments are not addressed to some people, but to all people who might listen. Not just the leaders of the people, the elite of the people, but to the poor and the oppressed. Not just to the men, but to the women as well. Not just to the adults, but to the children. Not just to one race, but to all races, setting out the blueprint for a just and equitable society in which all persons are granted the right to rest from their labors, to protection under the law, to a system of justice that strives for justice. This is not meant for some people, but for all people. God spoke all these words not to one person, not to one people, but to all people.

That is at least how our tradition understands it. This moment on the mountain, the moment of hearing God's voice, was the highest moment ever for a people and their God. A people gathered in community, hearing the voice, feeling the presence of their God and imprinting God's words on their hearts and souls. Never again would the Israelite community have such a moment of spiritual and moral rapture and perfection; and, of course, you know what happened next. Moses descends the mountain with the tablets written with God's own hand and sees the people dancing around the Golden Calf, and he smashes the tablets to pieces.

But what does Moses do? After his anger and his sadness begin to fade, he begins to climb again. Despite the failure and the setback, he ascends again. This time, the climb is even more difficult because he climbs alone; Joshua is not with him. This time the climb is even more difficult because he is climbing with the taste of defeat and disappointment and despair in his mouth. This time the climb is even more difficult because he is forced to cover ground he has already conquered to lift himself over obstacles he has already mastered. He knows the bitterness of having to climb over the same ground again, but onward he climbs until, once again, he has the precious tablets in his hands.

This story is instructive to us today, 50 years after the March on Washington and 46 years after the death of Dr. King. Looking back on those astonishing years, we realize that Dr. King and those who fought and marched at his side had conquered a mountain, climbed insurmountable obstacles, known every manner of suffering, including death and martyrdom, and yet they emerged from their climb up that mountain with precious rewards in their hands: the Voting Rights Act and the crumbling of open segregation and legal discrimination. No longer would the law support condemnation of one race to inferiority.

We emerged from the climb with the insistence that our society would no longer accept the presence of people living in lifelong poverty in the midst of wealth and bounty. Dr. King and those at his side climbed long, and they climbed hard, but they emerged cradling tangible gains. But then our society chose to build the Golden Calf, chose to worship at the altar of wealth and money and power, chose to ignore the poor and serve only the wealthy and the politically connected.

We have created a society in which the gap between the rich and poor is wider than it has ever been in our history, wider than in most industrialized nations. We have decided to create a society in which the chance of a poor person breaking out of poverty is less than it has ever been in our history as a nation. We have created a society in which more than 20 million children go to bed hungry every night. If 20 million children decided not to recite the Pledge of Allegiance tomorrow, we would be outraged, but 20 million children go to bed hungry, and no one says a word.

We are creating a society where more and more of our elected representatives feel empowered and free to say that the reason people are poor is that they are lazy and don't understand the virtue of hard work. What nerve, what chutzpah, to hear this from members of Congress who work, on average, 100 days a year!

We have created a society where, in many states, it is now harder for a poor person or a college student or an older person to vote than it was just a few years ago. We are creating a society where the Supreme Court has said there is no more racism; therefore, no more need for voter protection. We are creating a society where open hatred of a black president, hatred couched in racial terms, is now acceptable and common.

I'm not saying that life in America is worse than it was in 1963 or 1964. My father is from the South, and he tells me time and again that I cannot even begin to conceive what life was like then. "Son, until you have seen a water fountain or a movie entrance marked 'colored only,' you cannot know."

I am saying that as a society, having stood at the mountain and heard the call for justice and equality, heard it clearly and unmistakably, we allowed our society to build the Golden Calf, and now we have to climb the mountain again. And yes, as part of that climb, we have to surmount the same obstacles we thought that we had already conquered so long ago:

The right to vote freely.

The right to live without the curse of prejudice and discrimination.

The right to better ourselves economically.

The idea that we are all equal under the law, regardless of the wealth we possess, or the political influence we have bought.

So 50 years after the March on Washington, 46 years after Dr. King declared, "I've been to the mountaintop . . . and I've seen the Promised Land," we have to climb again. In some ways, the climb will be harder because we have tasted bitterness and setback, and we have seen obstacles painfully surmounted become obstacles again in our path.

But we will make it to the top because we know what awaits us at the summit – the same thing that awaited Dr. King. The reality of a country truly living by its creed: that all are created equal, that all are treated as equals, that justice serves every person with impartiality and fairness, and that we learn to see one another as equal children of God.

I want to end with a story told by the Holocaust survivor Elie Wiesel. He tells of a man who goes to the wicked city of Nineveh and walks the streets of Nineveh every day with a sign that says, "Repent of your wickedness." One day, a group of Ninevites comes to him and says, "Why do you walk? Don't you know you will never change them?" And he says, "I know. I walk now so that they will never change me."

So, even when the mountain seems impassable, climb anyway, if only so that you will not change. Even when the obstacles in your path seem too great, climb anyway, so you will not change. Even when the rocks and precipices are frightening and seem too high,

Climb anyway, so you will not change.

Climb anyway, and we will not change, and we will reach the summit.

Climb anyway, and we shall overcome.

CHAPTER FIFTEEN

The Future of Temple Emanu-El

Rabbi Douglas Sagal

Temple Emanu-El Senior Rabbi

FIRST LET ME SAY HOW DEEPLY APPRECIATIVE I AM OF ALL WHO PLAYED A ROLE IN making this volume a reality. From the exceptional writers to the meticulous editor to those indefatigable lay leaders who inspired the project, you are all worthy of great *hakarat hatov,* recognition and appreciation.

It falls now to me to outline my brief thoughts on where Temple Emanu-El will journey in the next decades.

I would like to suggest that Temple Emanu-El will pursue three interrelated paths.

One. There will be a priority given to creating a sense of sacred community, one precious relationship at a time. Our world is increasingly harsh, impersonal, and unforgiving. I believe the synagogue will return dramatically to its role of being the place of gathering, comfort, caring, and assistance. In some ways, we are returning to what we were at our founding, the central address of the Jewish community; the place of friendship, love, and support.

Two. There will be a priority given to education, both for adults and children. In many ways, we are living in a blessed time. Jews, and those who have connected themselves to the Jewish community, genuinely search for Jewish knowledge and skills. Temple Emanu-El will become a leader in education for the North American Jewish community.

Three. There will be a continuing return to authentic Jewish practice and traditions. Note that I am not saying a return to "Orthodoxy," for Orthodoxy is as much a product of the modern era as is Reform Judaism. No, I mean that increasingly no part of the Jewish tradition will be foreign to Temple Emanu-El. Whether it is Sabbath observance, dietary laws, or life cycle customs, we will reinterpret our ancient practices, imbuing them with the wisdom of the ethical life and with the importance of inclusiveness and love.

Above all, we will continue to be guided by the words carved on our façade, the words of the prophet Micah: *What does the Lord require of you? Only this — to do justly, to love mercy, and to walk humbly with your God.*

Postscript: As this book was going to press, the Pew Research Poll on Jewish Americans was released and garnered considerable attention in the Jewish community. ("A Portrait of Jewish Americans," Pew Research Religion & Public Life Project, October 2013; http://www.pewforum.org/2013/10/01/jewish-american-beliefs-attitudes-culture-survey/.) The following is an initial response to the data.

THE RECENT PEW RESEARCH STUDY, "A PORTRAIT OF JEWISH AMERICANS," PRESENTS the Jewish community with both good news and daunting challenges. Jewish self-identification is shifting; one in five Jews describe themselves as having "no religion." Not surprisingly, this statistic jumps to 32 percent among Millennials, the generation born beginning in 1980.

While many dwell on the negatives in the report, there are reasons for optimism. Looked at another way, the statistics tell us that 68 percent *do* identify as "Jews by religion." Moreover, 94 percent of American Jews, including those who identify as secular, or of "no religion," express pride in being Jewish and three-quarters say they have "a strong sense of belonging to the Jewish people."

The study finds that nearly three-quarters of the respondents see "leading an ethical life" as integral to Jewish identity, and more than half deem "working for justice and equality" essential. This tells us that the values we stand for are among those key to our Jewish future. The report also challenges us to find innovative ways, both inside and outside the walls of the synagogue, to connect Jews to the richness of our tradition and help them find meaning for their lives today.

What does the Pew Poll mean to those of us at Temple Emanu-El? To quote Rabbi Rick Jacobs, president of the URJ, "We should be concerned that the predominant religious affiliation of Millennials is 'none of the above'" (URJ Biennial Address 2013). We certainly need to think of new ways to engage young Jewish people in their 20s and 30s. However, we must also create better programming for those still in their teens that helps ensure a lifetime of affiliation and participation in Jewish life. It may be that more and more of our resources must be focused on youth and teen programming, helping to raise a new generation of Jewish youth for whom participating in Jewish life is vital and important.

We are living in a world and society where Jewish affiliation is not only a choice, but a choice among many competing and attractive possibilities for the next generation. We at Temple Emanu-El have an obligation, a sacred duty, to offer a Judaism so compelling and spiritually powerful that those who enter our doors, learn in our study halls, and worship in our sanctuary will find their lives forever transformed.

Author Biographies

Stephen E. Barcan

Stephen E. Barcan is an attorney with the law firm of Wilentz, Goldman & Spitzer, headquartered in Woodbridge, New Jersey. His practice areas include land use and environmental law, municipal law, and administrative law. In addition to major regional, national, and international clients, he represents religious institutions of all denominations. Past chairman of the New Jersey State Bar Association Land Use Section, Steve was named to the New Jersey Super Lawyers® list for the years 2005–13 and to Best Lawyers in America for the years 2012 and 2013. Steve is a member of the board of trustees of the Edison Arts Society and has served as president of Temple Emanu-El and the Westfield Symphony Orchestra.

Diana and Harold Cohen

Longtime Temple Emanu-El members dedicated to preserving its history and heritage, the Cohens have been the primary movers in the creation of this book.

Diana served as associate director, Professional Resource Development, for United Jewish Communities. Previous positions include associate executive director of the Jewish Federation of Central New Jersey and director of the Community Relations Council (CRC). Diana chaired the Temple Emanu-El Education and Social Action committees, served on the Federation board, directed the Cacciola Place tutoring project, and is currently a gallery educator at the Museum of Jewish Heritage and an ESL tutor.

A veteran of World War II, Harold was vice president of sales for a national manufacturing firm and currently operates his own business. He served as president of Temple Emanu-El, president of the Westfield Neighborhood Council, member of the Jewish Federation board, and chair of the UJA Westfield campaign. At the age of 83, he celebrated his second bar mitzvah. In 1976, the Cohens traveled to the Soviet Union on a secret mission to bring books, information, and expressions of worldwide support to Soviet activists, known as Refuseniks.

Helaine Gersten

A Westfield resident and Temple Emanu-El member for 40 years, Helaine Gersten chaired the Religious School and was a member of the Temple board of trustees for 10 years. A former art teacher, she also worked for the World Book Education Co. for 15 years as district manager, creating and presenting pre-school reading programs. Helaine was on the board of directors of the Westfield Symphony Orchestra for seven years as marketing and educational outreach chair. After 9/11 Helaine served as education programming consultant for the Mental Health Association.

Rabbi Arnold S. Gluck

Rabbi Gluck has served as rabbi of Temple Beth-El of Hillsborough, New Jersey, since 1991. After receiving rabbinic ordination in 1983, Rabbi Gluck was Associate Rabbi at Temple Emanu-El of Westfield. From 1986 to 1991, he lived in Haifa, Israel, where he served the Reform Movement's Leo Baeck Education Center as director of the Lehrman Community Center and rabbi of Congregation Ohel Avraham.

Rabbi Gluck has served on the URJ/CCAR Joint Commission on Outreach and Caring Community, co-authoring its Taste of Judaism program. He was the founding coordinator of the Beit Din for Conversion of the New Jersey Association of Reform Rabbis and was a member of the CCAR Conversion committee and CCAR Task Force on the Challenge of Intermarriage for the Reform Rabbi. Rabbi Gluck currently serves on the CCAR Responsa committee and chairs the CCAR Israel committee.

Mike Hamerman

Mike Hamerman and his wife Nora joined Temple Emanu-El in 1978. Mike has been a member of Men's Club since 1978 and has held many offices, including serving as Men's Club president from 2004–06. He also served as a teacher in the Temple Emanu-El Religious School and as advisor to the Junior Youth Group from 1987–1996. In addition, Mike is an active member of the Shabbat Morning Minyan. He is a retired schoolteacher, having taught language arts and reading in the New York City public school system for 35 years.

Barbara Z. Koppel

Barbara Koppel received a BA degree in English from the University of Massachusetts at Amherst and an MA in comparative literature from the City University of New York (CUNY) Graduate Center. She has taught public school in Boston, Massachusetts, and in Elizabeth, New Jersey, and was an adjunct instructor in English at Kean University. Barbara also taught high school English at Bruriah High School, the girls' division of the Jewish Educational Center yeshiva in Elizabeth, for many years. She taught in the Temple Emanu-El Religious School and chaired the Religious School committee in the 1990s. Barbara has worked for various arms of the Reform Movement, including the URJ, CCAR, and WRJ, and was project coordinator for *The Torah: A Women's Commentary*, published by the URJ Press and WRJ. Barbara and her husband, Robert Koppel, the executive director of the Reform Pension Board and past president of Emanu-El, are longtime members of the Temple. Their daughter, Rabbi Elisa Koppel, is currently associate rabbi at Temple Beth-El in San Antonio, Texas.

Rabbi Charles A. Kroloff

Rabbi Kroloff served as senior rabbi of Temple Emanu-El for 36 years, from 1966 until his retirement in 2002, when he was named rabbi emeritus. On his retirement, the new educational wing of the Temple was named the Rabbi Charles A. Kroloff Center for Jewish Learning. Currently vice president for Special Projects of HUC-JIR, Rabbi Kroloff remains active in the Westfield area through leadership of Temple Emanu-El's "I Have a Dream" program and as president of the Westfield Foundation.

A graduate of Yale University, Rabbi Kroloff was president of the CCAR, the largest international organization of rabbis in the world. Before coming to Westfield, he was assistant rabbi at Temple Israel, Boston, and rabbi of Community Reform Temple, Westbury, New York. A past president of ARZA, Rabbi Kroloff was a member of the governing boards of the Jewish Agency, HUC-JIR, and the URJ. He was a founder of the Interfaith Council for the Homeless of Union County and, following retirement, interim rabbi at Stephen Wise Free Synagogue, New York City. Rabbi Kroloff is the author of *When Elijah Knocks, A Religious Response to Homelessness*; *54 Ways You Can Help the Homeless*; and *Reform Judaism: A Jewish Way of Life*.

Terry Kroloff, PhD

Over the past 55 years, Terry has had many varied and extended experiences in Israel, along with her husband, Rabbi Charles Kroloff. She has visited the country on at least 20 occasions, studied at the Hebrew University, led tours, owned a home, and lived in the country for extended periods of time. Following her undergraduate studies at Wellesley College and the University of Cincinnati, she earned a PhD in English literature from Drew University. Formerly CEO of Corporate Press Inc., an editing and printing company producing newsletters and other publications for corporations and non-profit organizations, Terry has also been an adjunct professor of English at Fairleigh Dickinson, Drew, Rutgers, and Kean Universities.

Rabbi Ellen Lewis

Rabbi Lewis, the second Temple Emanu-El member to become a rabbi, was ordained in 1980 by HUC-JIR. She was rabbi of the Jewish Center of Northwest New Jersey in Washington, New Jersey, until 2013, when she was named rabbi emerita. She is also a psychoanalyst with offices in New Jersey and New York. Rabbi Lewis has a particular interest in working with rabbis and cantors in therapy and in professional supervision. She received her analytical training in New York at the Center for Modern Psychoanalytic Studies and is on the faculty of the Academy of Clinical and Applied Psychoanalysis. A graduate of Brown University, Rabbi Lewis is also certified as a Fellow in the American Association of Pastoral Counselors. She is widely published and a frequent lecturer on various topics related to both Judaism and psychoanalysis.

Rabbi Jill Maderer

Rabbi Maderer is associate rabbi, Congregation Rodeph Shalom, Philadelphia, where she has served since her ordination by HUC-JIR in 2001. Rabbi Maderer works to build community, especially through study and ritual. She coordinates opportunities to engage through Adult Education, the Multi-Generational Contemporary High Holy Day services, Families with Young Children, Tot Shabbat, and the Early Learning Center. She is also a member of the executive board of the Philadelphia Board of Rabbis and the board of Kehillah of Center City. Jill's Judaism was shaped by her parents, Temple Emanu-El — her hometown congregation, her youth group involvement, and her undergraduate experience. During her years at Temple Emanu-El, Jill served as social action vice president of youth group and then of JFTY. She graduated from Brandeis University with a major in Near Eastern and Judaic studies and minored in women's studies and peace and conflict studies.

Cantor Martha Novick

Senior cantor at Temple Emanu-El since 1986, Cantor Novick received a BS in music performance and an MA in music education from New York University. She also received a Bachelor of Sacred Music from HUC-JIR School of Sacred Music, where she was invested as cantor in May of 1983. She has served on the faculty of the School of Sacred Music and the Jewish Theological Seminary of America, Miller Cantorial School.

Cantor Novick has performed leading roles in opera for the Metropolitan Opera Association, the National Shakespeare Theatre, CBS and PBS Television, WNYC, the Center for New Music in New York, and the Liederkranz Opera Workshop. She has been soloist with the Jerusalem Symphony, the Brooklyn Philharmonia Chorus, Musica Hebraica, Sela, and the Hebrew Arts Chorale. Cantor Novick has served on the board of the American Conference of Cantors, the Commission on Synagogue Music, the advisory board and review board of Transcontinental Music Publishing, and currently serves as vice president of the American Society for Jewish Music. She has the distinction of being the first female cantor to perform in a traditional cantorial concert in a major concert hall in New York. She has also made a CD of Yiddish art songs for the Milken Foundation Archives of Twentieth Century American Jewish Composers and a CD of High Holiday Music for Transcontinental Music Publishing.

Jacqui Rose

A native New Yorker, Jacqui was raised with a strong commitment to Jewish values and social action. An educator of the hearing impaired in the Bloomfield school system for many years, Jacqui originated mainstream programs for disabled children attending New Jersey public schools and served on the Governor's Task Force on Employment of People with Disabilities. At Temple Emanu-El, Jacqui chaired the Social Action committee where she initiated the Temple's participation in the Interfaith Council for the Homeless Hospitality Network. In partnership with St. Mark's

Episcopal Church in Plainfield, she was also instrumental in the creation of ARK, the Association for Rehabilitation with Kindness, winner of the URJ Kovler Award for Black-Jewish Relations. Also on the national level, Jacqui was a member of the URJ Commission on Social Action and Task Force for the Disabled. Locally, together with her husband Steve, Jacqui co-chaired the first Super Sunday event for the Jewish Federation. One of her greatest pleasures is the honor of reading *Maftir Yonah* on Yom Kippur afternoon.

Rabbi Douglas Sagal

Senior rabbi at Temple Emanu-El since 2002, Rabbi Sagal received his rabbinic ordination from HUC-JIR. He is a graduate of Wesleyan University and the Yale Divinity School, where he won the annual award for outstanding preaching, the only rabbi ever to do so. He is the author of several articles on preaching and biblical interpretation, as well as other subjects. Formerly a faculty member of the Academy for Jewish Religion in New York City, he has also been a guest lecturer at HUC-JIR and is profiled extensively in the best-selling book, *Today I am a Boy: A Memoir* by David Hays.

Rabbi Joel E. Soffin

Rabbi Soffin served as the student rabbi/youth director at Temple Emanu-El from 1973–76 under the mentorship of Rabbi Kroloff. After spending the next three years as assistant rabbi at Temple Beth Israel of West Hartford, Connecticut, he became the rabbi of Temple Shalom in Succasunna, New Jersey, and served there from 1979 to 2006. Upon his retirement, he created the Jewish Helping Hands Foundation to continue his worldwide social action efforts.

Rabbi Lennard R. Thal

Rabbi Thal most recently served as interim director of Rabbinical Placement (2009-2011) and is also senior vice president emeritus of the URJ. He served first as vice president and then senior vice president from 1995 until 2008, as well as chief development officer. Rabbi Thal was regional director of the URJ's Pacific Southwest Council from 1982 to 1995, associate dean of HUC-JIR, Los Angeles Campus, from 1973 to 1982, and has been visiting rabbi for the High Holy Days at the United Hebrew Congregation of Singapore since 1993.

Rabbi Thal received an AB from Princeton University, a JD from Stanford University Law School, and an MAHL, rabbinic ordination, and DD from HUC-JIR. He is the recipient of numerous academic and community awards and has a lengthy and distinguished list of organizational affiliations.

Bernard and Lynn Turiel

Born on the island of Rhodes, Bernard Turiel came to the United States after World War II at the age of 11. He earned his undergraduate and law school degrees at New York University. Bernie worked at the Federal Trade Commission in New York before transferring to Washington DC, where he met Lynn. A native of North Carolina, Lynn had moved to Washington for a job at the National Security Agency after graduating from the University of North Carolina. They moved to Westfield in 1966, where Bernie established a law practice. Now retired, Bernie and Lynn volunteer with the Mostly Music organization.

Rabbi Jeffrey Weill

Rabbi Weill is the rabbi of Ezra Habonim, the Niles Township Jewish Congregation in Skokie, Illinois, and a member of the HUC-JIR President's Rabbinic Council. He also served for five years first as an assistant, then as associate rabbi at Temple Beth-El in Northbrook, Illinois. A graduate of Brandeis University, Rabbi Weill also holds a law degree from American University. The former Emanu-El youth group social action vice president spent 10 years in the Jewish non-profit world, working most recently for the Jewish Community Relations Council of the Jewish United Fund of Metropolitan Chicago, where he focused on domestic and international issues that affect the Jewish community. Before coming to Chicago, he was deputy director of the American Jewish Committee Human Rights Institute in New York. After changing careers, he was ordained in 2007 at HUC-JIR, serving as Temple Emanu-El student rabbi from 2004 to 2005.

Rabbi Eric H. Yoffie

Rabbi Yoffie is president emeritus of the URJ. Installed as president in June 1996, Rabbi Yoffie led the Reform Movement in new directions, moving congregational life toward greater attention to Torah study and adult Jewish literacy. He spearheaded a major expansion of the URJ summer camping program and led worship initiatives to help congregations become "houses in which we pray with joy," rethink Shabbat morning worship, and foster Shabbat observance among individual Reform Jews. Rabbi Yoffie has been a pioneer in interfaith relations and launched movement-wide dialogue programs with both Christians and Muslims. He has also been deeply involved in issues of social justice and community concern and has worked tirelessly on behalf of the Jewish State and the rights of Reform Jews in Israel, where he meets frequently with elected officials.

Raised in Worcester, Massachusetts, Rabbi Yoffie was ordained at HUC-JIR in 1974 and served congregations in Lynbrook, New York, and Durham, North Carolina, before joining the Union in 1980, eventually serving as executive director of ARZA. A graduate of Brandeis University, Rabbi Yoffie and his wife Amy are longtime residents of Westfield and members of Temple Emanu-El.

Rabbi Mary Zamore

The editor of the critically acclaimed *The Sacred Table: Creating a Jewish Food Ethic* (CCAR Press, 2011), Rabbi Zamore serves as rabbi of the Jewish Center of Northwest New Jersey, Washington, New Jersey. Until 2013, she was the associate rabbi of Temple B'nai Or of Morristown, New Jersey. Ordained by HUC-JIR in New York in 1997, she has served Temple Emanu-El as student intern, and assistant and associate rabbi (1996–2002). Rabbi Zamore is active in the CCAR and Women's Rabbinic Network (WRN). She is a past co-president of WRN (2008–09), a past editor of the CCAR Newsletter (2000–01), and served as a CCAR board member, representing the WRN (2008–12). She is a blogger for the *Huffington Post*. Rabbi Zamore and her family reside in Westfield.

Acknowledgments

Tis book began as a celebration of significant milestones in the life of Temple Emanu-El: our sixtieth anniversary, the fiftieth anniversary of Rabbi Kroloff's rabbinic ordination at Hebrew Union College, and Rabbi Sagal's decade of continuing leadership. What emerged, as Rabbi Yoffie's introduction captures so beautifully, is a tribute to Emanu-El's unique leadership in the Reform Jewish Movement, even as it reflects the development of liberal Judaism in America since 1950. We are proud to be a part of this history and look forward to continuing innovation and contributions to Jewish life.

Many people were instrumental in the creation of this book. We owe a great debt to Evelyn Averick, who set a high standard with her earlier history. We remember with deep affection Adam Bengal, former Temple Emanu-El president and managing editor at KTAV Publishing House, who guided us through the early stages of preparation.

Thanks to our dedicated authors and to those who helped us with research, personal memories, insights, and interviews. Their contributions are invaluable. We particularly wish to acknowledge the support of the Temple Emanu-El clergy; Executive Director Carolyn Shane; archivists Anne Glasser and Henriann "Honi" Robins; and Professor Jonathan Sarna of Brandeis University.

Special thanks to the Temple Emanu-El Men's Club and Sisterhood for their support.

So many people have been helpful and supportive with personal memories, photos, and research. Our sincere apologies for any names we may have inadvertently omitted.

We want to recognize the original committee members who conducted the initial research and encouraged us to produce this collection of essays: Adam Bengal, Phyllis Buchsbaum, Joe Fox, Gail Friedman, Charlotte Gelfand, Helaine Gersten, Sally Gilbert, Anne Glasser, Ann and Shelly Glickman, Susan Good, Susan Jacobson, Barbara Koppel, Terry and Rabbi Charles Kroloff, Bea Reiss, Gene Rosner, Jerry Schwartz, Selma and Harold Wasserman, and Susan and Lowell Yemin.

Others who also provided invaluable research and personal memories include Andy Baron, Jean Benisch, Arlene Burstein, Shirley Cowan, Rabbi Susan Friedman, Stanley Gersch, Brad Gerstle, Ellen Gottdenker, Rabbi Deborah Joselow, Zelda Kahn, Janice Kessler, Terri Klass, Rabbi Elisa Koppel, Eileen Nathanson, Vivian Newmark, Bea Reiss, Lucille Rosenberg, Steve Rosenberg, Tamara (Coty) Ruben, Marci Schoenbach, Carolyn Shane, Rabbi Howard Sommer, Cantor Jill Spasser, Miriam Silver Verga, and Elaine Weill.

Thanks also to Reform Jewish leaders who contributed their insights: Jan Epstein, Rosanne Selfon, Cantor Benjie Ellen Schiller, and Rabbis Marla Feldman, Shirley Idelson, Jan Katzew, Jeffrey K. Salkin, and Michael White.

It has been an honor for us to lead this effort with so many dedicated, talented people. We hope the generations that follow will build on the strong foundation of study, prayer, and social justice we sought to establish from those early years continuing into the present.

Kein Ye'hi Ratzon

Diana and Harold Cohen

Rabbis and Cantors:
Temple Emanu-El Graduates

The following rabbis and cantors ordained and invested by HUC-JIR, the Jewish Theological Seminary of America, Academy for Jewish Religion, and Aleph: Alliance for Jewish Renewal have all been part of the Temple Emanu-El family.

Rabbi Rachel Ackerman
Rabbi Daniel Alexander
Rabbi Marcus L. Burstein
Cantor Jennifer Robin
  Kanarek Cahn
Rabbi Susan Friedman
Rabbi Elisa Koppel
Rabbi Ellen Jay Lewis

Rabbi Charles Lightner
Rabbi Helga Newmark
Rabbi Jill Maderer
Rabbi Jacqueline Tattenbaum
  Satlow
Rabbi Jeffrey Segall
Rabbi Jonathan Seidel
Cantor Jill Spasser

Rabbi David Wechsler-Azen
Rabbi Jeffrey Weill
Rabbi Mara Judd Young

Temple Emanu-El Rabbis and Cantors

Rabbis

Ezra Spicehandler 1951–53
David Raab 1953–55
Jack Stern Jr. 1955–62
Azriel Grishman 1962–64
Bernard Honan 1964–66
Charles A. Kroloff 1966–2002
Charles A. Kroloff, rabbi emeritus
  2002–present
Douglas B. Sagal 2002–present

Cantors

Don Decker 1960–86
Don Gurney, interim cantor 1981–82
Don Decker, cantor emeritus
  1986–present
Martha Novick 1986–present

Assistant/Associate Rabbis

Howard F. Seldin-Sommer 1978–82
Arnold S. Gluck★ 1983–86
Mark Lloyd Disick 1986–91
Deborah A. Joselow 1992–98
Mary L. Zamore★ 1997–2002
Renee B. Goldberg Edelman
  1997–2003
Jennifer Clayman 2003–08
Leah Rose Doberne-Schor 2005–10
Erin R. Glazer 2009–present
Sarah Smiley 2011–present

★Also served as student rabbi

Student Rabbis

Lennard Thal 1970–73
Joel E. Soffin 1973–76
Warren Stone 1976–78
Jeffrey Weill 2004–05

Assistant Cantor

Michelle Rubel 2012–present

Cantorial Assistant

Ronni Pressman 2007–12

Student Cantors

Marshall Glatzer 1950–52
Paul Silbersher 1952–55
Martin Rosen 1955–58
Sidney Keiser 1958–59
Lewis Appleton 1959–60
Jaime Shpall 1995–97
Jonathan Comisar 1997–98
Rosalie Will 1998–99
Leon Sher 1999–2001

Carrie Brawer 2001–03
Elena Schwartz 2003–07

Temple Emanu-El Presidents

Temple Presidents

David Schimmel 1950–52
Nathan Stritzler 1952–53
Karl Millman 1953–54
Harry Jaffe 1954–55
Nathaniel M. Cohen 1955–57
Melvin Grabel 1957–59
J. Leonard Wilson 1959–61
Isaac Daniels 1961–63
Sidney C. Mele 1963–65
Dr. Francis Lehr 1965–66
Seymour Krueger 1966–68
Samuel Mallor 1968–70
Gabriel Malkin 1970–72
Harold A. Cohen 1972–74
Alan Goldstein 1974–76
David Kabakow 1976–78
David Bregman 1978–80
Zelda Kahn 1980–82
Eileen Nathanson 1982–84
Stephen Barcan 1984–86
Eugene Rosner 1986–88
Robert M. Koppel 1988–90
Elaine Weill 1990–92
William Maderer 1992–94

Dr. Stanley Gersch 1994–96
Phyllis N. Buchsbaum 1996-98
Adam Bengal 1998–2000
Stephen Rosenberg 2000–02
Terri Klass 2002–04
Marci Schoenbach 2004–06
Darren Schulman 2006–08
Gail Friedman 2008–10
Shepard Federgreen 2010–12
David Buckman 2012–present

Sisterhood Presidents

Ruth Millman 1951–53
Lillian Lerman 1953–55
Anne Shapiro 1955–56
Bette Morris 1956–57
Kiki Kass 1957–59
Joyce Grabel Tischler 1959–61
Lilyan Weiss 1961–63
Lorraine Gershenfeld 1963–64
Sylvia Sommerfield 1964–66
Charlotte Gold 1966–68
Zelda Kahn 1968–69
Rita Kessler 1969–71
Eileen Nathanson 1971–73
Seena Feinsmith 1973–75

Agnes Faber 1975–77
Phyllis Reiss 1977–78
Daryl Worth 1978–80
Sherri Stern 1980–82
Sylvia Cohen 1982–84
Irene Katz 1984–86
Deena Ochs 1986–88
Arlene Burstein 1988–90
Pamela Bernstein 1990–92
Janet Kanarek 1992–94
Andrea Wiener 1994–96
Margaret Kahn 1996–98
Nanci Pompan 1998–2000
Jacqueline Bass 2000–02
Cheryl Oberman 2002–04
Susan Schuman 2004–06
Pamela Bernstein 2006–07
Gail Erlich 2007–08
Sharon Zydney 2008–12
Suzanne Rosenthal 2012–present

Men's Club Presidents

Fred Ehrich 1954–55
Melvin Grabel 1955–56
Jerry Craft 1956–57
J. Leonard Wilson 1957–58

Jack Kutzenco 1958–60
Dr. Francis Lehr 1960–62
Edward I. Lewis 1962–64
Harold J. Weiss 1964–66
Bernard Heller 1966–68
Dr. Marvin Fein 1968–69
Richard Lane 1969–71
Jerry Krupnick 1971–73
Martin Goldstein 1973–75
Simon Kaplan 1975–77
Harold Kahn 1977–78

Jerome Linder 1978–80
Melvin Cohen 1980–82
Louis Tischler 1982–84
Joseph Indick (honorary) 1985
Herbert Ross 1985–86
Richard Gordon 1986–88
Robert Mansfeld 1988–89
Lewis Ochs 1989–92
Dr. Ivan Jacobs 1992–94
Dr. Julian Burstein 1994–95
Dr. Ivan Jacobs 1995–96

Martin Spector 1996–98
Jonathon Bass 1998–2000
David M. Schulman 2000–02
Jonathon Bass 2002–04
Michael Hamerman 2004–06
Andrew Baron 2006–08
Dr. David Gelber 2008–10
Stanley Biner 2010–12
Marc Epstein 2012–present

Donors

Special thanks to our donors and supporters who helped make this volume a reality.

Steve and Bettye Barcan
Phyllis Buchsbaum
David and Cheryl Buckman
Arnold and Jaclyn Civins
Carol Cohen and Morrie Acker
Harold and Diana Cohen
Howard and Sylvia Cohen
Susan Coren
Warren and Mitzi Eisenberg
Andrew and Pamela
    Federbusch
Lawrence and Cyndy Fields
Stephen and Marci Fisher
Rabbis John Fishman and
    Jennifer Clayman
Dr. Jerome and Diane Forman
Eric and Gail Friedman
Drs. Robert and Susan
    Fuhrman
Richard and Karen Furst

Peter and Toby Ganz
Dr. David and Joan Gelber
Dr. Gerald Glasser
Lawrence and Cynthia
    Goldman
Richard and Faith Gordon
Ronald and Debra
    Greenberg Heitner
Saul Heitner and Laurie
    Goldsmith
Edward Israelow and Arlene
    Gardner
David and Debra Judd
Harold and Zelda Kahn
Richard and Terri Klass
Myron and Rea Kolski
Robert and Barbara Koppel
Rabbi Charles and
    Dr. Terry Kroloff
Dr. Neal and Virginia Luppescu

Harlan and Susan Martin
Randy and Randye Masel
Paul and Amy Mesches
Cantor Martha T. Novick
Dr. Jeffrey and Eleanor Peris
Nanci Pompan
Dr. Esther Rose
Stephen and Lucille Rosenberg
Rabbi Doug Sagal
Michael and Marci Schoenbach
Darren and Harriet Schulman
Daniel and Susan Stern
Joyce Tischler
Donald and Elaine Weill
Lowell and Susan Yemin
Men's Club of Temple
    Emanu-El
Yahrzeit Fund of Temple
    Emanu-El